WHY IS THE
BUDDHA
SMILING?

WHY IS THE
BUDDHA
SMILING?

mindfulness as a means of bringing
calm and insight to your life

MARK MAGILL

FAIR WINDS
PRESS
GLOUCESTER, MASSACHUSETTS

Published in 2003 in the U.S.A. by

Fair Winds Press
33 Commercial Street
Gloucester, MA 01930

www.fairwindspress.com

Library of Congress Cataloging-in-Publication Data available

ISBN 1-59233-019-3

10 9 8 7 6 5 4 3 2 1

Printed and bound in Canada

Cover illustration: Johnny Pau
Cover photograph: The Image Bank
Designed and produced for Godsfield Press by
The Bridgewater Book Company

acknowledgments

I would like to acknowledge Brenda Rosen for suggesting
this book and arranging for its publication.
I wish to thank Sat Chuen Hon for suggesting a wider scope for this book
and urging me not to waste a tree. I hope I have not.
Thanks go to Marielle Boncou-Segal for permission to quote her late husband,
William Segal, toward the end of this book.
I would also like to thank Susan Schwarzwald, Werner Bargsten,
and their daughter, Anika, for giving me a few days of salt-sea air
to cure the last chapters of this book in their island retreat.
I want to thank Sherry Holzman for her unstinting friendship
and for the rare quality of unsparingly honest criticism.
And, finally, I want to thank Blanche Baker from the bottom of my heart
for her unfailing encouragement during the days and hours of this work.

I sincerely hope this book will be
of some help to those who happen to read it.
Whatever its faults, they are entirely my own.
Whatever its benefits, they are entirely due to the
wisdom and kindness of my teachers.

contents

preface

I had been looking for a teacher for a long while. I attended a number of teachings and retreats, sometimes sitting for days on end with the usual woes of a Westerner's knees. All the while I was asking myself, "Is he the one? Is she the one?" When you're uncertain, anything is possible and everything is in question. You're never quite sure, so you weigh the pros and cons, hoping for a sign.

Traditional Tibetan teachings list a number of qualities to look for in a teacher:

- He should know more than you.
- He should have tamed his negative emotions.
- He should be compassionate.
- He should be well-behaved and well-balanced.
- He should have true understanding and experience of the teachings and be able to present them in a clear and comprehensible fashion according to the level of the student.
- He should be able to prove the points he teaches.
- He should have perseverance.
- He should be able to endure a little hardship.

The teachings stress that you must decide for yourself if this person has these qualities. Such a person will never declare outright, "I am your teacher, you are my student." If they do, it's time to head for the exit. It's up to you to decide if the teacher is right for you.

Still I struggled along. I voiced my ongoing questions to a friend, who would repeat the same line each time she heard my complaint:

"When the student is ready, the teacher will come." "Yes, but how will I know?" I would ask. "When the student is ready, the teacher will come," was her steady reply.

Then one day someone comes along and you simply say, "Oh, there he is."

It was a wintry night fit for Tibetans, not all that many years ago, when I first crossed Gehlek Rimpoche's path.

When I look back, I have to say we hit it off right away, if you can say that about a Tibetan lama and a volunteer firefighter from upstate New York. I found someone who spoke not only from an extraordinary wealth of knowledge, but from kind and compassionate experience. But a teacher like Rimpoche provides something else. He provides an example.

In the years before he escaped from the Chinese occupation, Rimpoche was educated in the great monasteries of Tibet. His teachers included two of the Dalai Lama's own instructors. Although he was from a noble family in Lhasa, a nephew of the Thirteenth Dalai Lama, Rimpoche fled his country without a penny to his name. Yet he brought something that fills me with gratefulness beyond measure. He brought the teachings.

I've since spent a fair amount of time in Rimpoche's company, working with him on various projects or just hanging out drinking tea while the sun moves from east to west. He is kind, thoughtful, and extraordinarily generous without a shred of sentimentality. He loves to joke and his nimble command of his adopted language keeps me laughing. His company is a pleasure.

Through Rimpoche, I have had the good fortune to meet other teachers of great generosity and patience. Anything of sense I have to say in this book, I owe to the kindness of Rimpoche and my other teachers.

introduction

I've been keeping bees for the past ten years. When I started out, I was stung a lot. There's nothing unusual about that. It is part of the business of beekeeping.

At first, it was quite painful. I tried my best to avoid it, but I enjoyed working with the bees, following the rhythm of the seasons along with them. The bees gather nectar from the flowers and bring it back to the hive, where they transform it into honey. By the end of the summer they have concentrated the essence of a season's blossoms.

I grew so I no longer minded the stings. They were still just as painful, but because of my appreciation of beekeeping, I didn't mind the pain. It was part of the process, I thought, the price to be paid for working with them. Honeybees live solely by gathering the nectar and pollen from flowers. Unlike wasps, which hunt and kill other insects and can sting repeatedly, a honeybee dies when it stings. They will sting in defense of the hive, but they give up their lives in the defense. I began to understand that I was not being stung capriciously or for spite. When I looked more closely, I realized that in every instance I was stung because I had made a mistake—from something as simple as thoughtlessly leaning against a bee resting on my pant leg, to the more egregious act of opening the hive on a sunny day in the fall after the first frost.

The bees were teaching me. On warm, sunny days in the summer when nectar is in abundance, the bees scarcely mind the intrusion of a curious beekeeper. But on a similar day in the fall, after the frost has killed the flowers, the bees become intensely defensive of the honey that must feed them through the winter. But what was a painful lesson for me was a far more costly one for them. In order to avoid pain for myself and suffering for them, I had to become a more thoughtful beekeeper.

I continued to work with the bees, but I had to look more carefully into my actions and their consequences. It required a better understanding of the nature of the bees and the conditions of the moment. It required me to act mindfully.

learning lessons

It's been a while since I was stung. I still work the bees each summer and harvest the honey each fall. No doubt I will make a mistake and be stung again. But now I know the cost of the lesson and the compelling reason to learn.

I believe it is like that for most of us. We try our best, but we make mistakes with our friends, lovers, parents, and children. In spite of our best intentions and our intense desire for happiness, again and again we discover we have brought suffering to ourselves and others. Who hasn't experienced tears, a broken heart, a lost friendship, confusion, misunderstanding, pain? We find ourselves in painful situations with consequences we had no intention of causing. What is wrong? This is no small question. At its heart lies the cause of our problems.

Everyone of us seeks happiness. All of us would like to be free from suffering. Every living creature shares this wish. Even tiny ants run from the ant spray to be free from suffering. For us, freedom from suffering is happiness. It is more powerful than the wish for life itself. In the unfortunate case of suicide, a person is willing to die in order to be free from suffering. We say it all the time when someone dies—"At least he didn't suffer"—meaning death is preferable to suffering.

the path to freedom

Twenty-five hundred years ago, an Indian prince of the Sakya clan sat down at the foot of a tree in a place known as Bodh Gaya. He had taken a vow that he would not rise again until he had discovered a path to freedom from the sufferings that beset the world. He had left his palace six years earlier in a quest for understanding. He endured many austerities in his search, wandering from place to place, seeking the truth from various teachers, but none satisfied him with an answer he believed would free all beings from suffering.

And so he had made his way to the foot of the bodhi tree. It was the evening of the full moon, in the fourth month of the year. He remained seated there in deep contemplation throughout the night. As he sat, he was beset with fearful apparitions. Demons appeared hurling spears, arrows, and fiery weapons at him. Through the power of his compassion, he transformed these fears into a rain of flowers. Then he was tempted by an array of earthly delights. Unswayed by these distractions, he deepened his concentration on his goal. Through the power of wisdom, he saw the true nature of reality—both the cause of suffering and the path to its cessation. As the morning star appeared, the Buddha rose at last from meditation. He had discovered the way to freedom.

Shakyamuni Buddha made the truth of suffering his first teaching after he attained enlightenment under the bodhi tree. His message is that we experience all kinds of suffering in our lives—not just the fundamental suffering of birth, aging, illness, and death. We also suffer the pain of separation from loved ones, association with unpleasant persons, not getting the objects we crave, losing the things we are attached to, and the suffering of desire itself. As long as we are governed by the negative emotions of craving and attachment that arise from a fundamental misunderstanding about the true source of happiness, we remain prisoners of suffering.

I believe the teachings have endured because they reveal an understanding of our human nature and the conditions we face. We all share a wish for happiness and freedom from suffering. We face obstacles that prevent us from fulfilling that wish. But there is a way to overcome those obstacles.

If you look carefully at images of the Buddha, you will find a smile—subtle and enigmatic, perhaps, yet present nonetheless. Why is the Buddha smiling? Because he discovered there is a path to freedom. It is a path available to everyone who is determined to make the effort to follow it. The path begins with mindfulness.

part one

M I N D F

discovering mindfulness

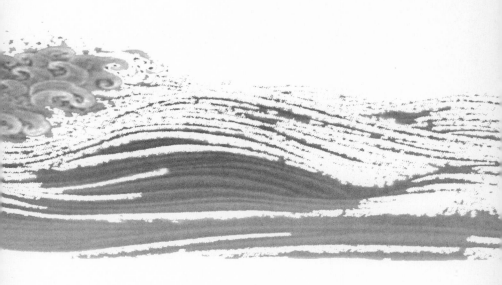

the deer at the watering hole

chapter 1

Our nervous systems are naturally wired

*to respond to **adversity**, but society lulls*

*us to sleep with a sense of **comfort** and*

***security**. How can we regain the alertness*

of the deer at the watering hole?

It is twilight. The deer have gathered at the watering hole, a low spot on the broad savannah surrounded by acacia trees. They drink, but they remain at the height of alertness. Their survival depends on it. All around, they feel the eyes of predators watching in the gathering dark. Nature has graced them with exquisite sensitivity and the gift of speed. They must use their senses to the fullest if they are to survive the relentless dance between predator and prey. It is, perhaps, a million years ago.

In a time much closer to our own, the descendants of those same deer graze in an enclosed park, protected from all danger. Attendants dole out grain, on which the deer feed from metal troughs. Their water comes from a spigot with little chance of running dry. The peril of the wild has been replaced by comfort and freedom from fear. Within their enclosure, they have become tame.

We are endowed with those same senses. We share a similar legacy. In our desire for comfort and freedom from fear, we, too, have become tame. But this sense of security comes at a price. We are lulled by it, thinking nothing untoward can befall us, at least not right now. The pursuit of happiness and freedom from suffering are natural. But have we really found them within the enclosure? Are we really free?

The deer in the park are protected by the fence as long as the fence holds. In the meantime, no longer wary of the lurking danger, they have become easy prey. They have relinquished the alertness that sustained them so well in the wild.

It may not be too much to say that we, too, have relinquished our pristine awareness. In its place, we tend to dwell in the past or daydream of the future, drifting hazily back and forth. In lighter moments, we have pleasant memories and happy anticipations. However, these cheerful thoughts are soon followed by their surly partners, regret and anxiety. The thoughts themselves bring both satisfaction and worry. It is an equation of happiness and suffering that governs our actions from our first cry to our last breath.

This rise and fall of thought would be of very little consequence in itself except that we are held so spellbound. We are drawn to pleasant thoughts and repelled by painful ones, yet we are equally captivated by both.

If I look carefully just now, I see I am drawn to the pleasant thought of meeting my lover in the coming evening. I imagine we'll walk at sunset on the high cliffs above the river. The light will be majestic. We'll hold hands and revel in each other's presence. We'll speak of our future, of the child we hope to have.

Then another character of thought creeps in. Will the child be healthy? How will I support this new person? Writing about mindfulness doesn't pay much. Will I meet the publisher's deadline? Do I have anything worth saying? Maybe I should take a break and get something to eat. I could check on the bees. A bear came through a few weeks ago and damaged the hives. Better walk up the hill just in case. Anything to avoid the work at hand.

Where is all this rambling taking place? Certainly not on the sunlit cliffs, in the baby's bright nursery, or in the buzzing apiary. I'm rummaging around a dim attic upstairs, sorting through likes and dislikes, hopes and fears—none of which is present in the here and now. They are all in my mind. It is this mind that governs my actions. Those actions, taking place in the present, are what will shape my future happiness or misery. Is this swaying between imagined pleasures and worries making the best use of the mind's capacity? Is it charting the best course for freedom?

If I look carefully, I see that I am little different from a man lying in bed, unconscious in his dreams. My thoughts wander, lurching this way and that, like those of a sleeper coursing through a dreamscape. What is it that captures my attention? It is this flickering desire for happiness and the avoidance of pain? The imagined sunset shared with my lover holds the promise of pleasure. The burden of earning my keep brings the prospect of worry.

Can this mind be put to better use? Can my attention take on a different character, one not so easily scattered by every little breeze of like and dislike? Can I focus on the work at hand? What is that work? I believe it is to awaken to my true condition. I need to gain awareness of my actions in all regards. I need to see how my shortsighted idea of what will bring me happiness is actually working against me. I need to see the deluded nature of my sleep. Otherwise, how can I hope to help myself? How can I possibly help others? Without the proper attention, I stand to make a fair botch of all my well-intentioned efforts.

There is definitely a way out of this dilemma. But it requires an effort. Just as with any work of quality, the business of life requires our attention.

The word *Buddha* literally means "the awakened one." This is hardly an accident. To awaken to our potential, we must repeatedly confront ourselves with awareness. This is no small task. But the Buddha was a human being with the same capacity as ourselves. Yet he achieved total illumination while most of us are still trying to make our way in the dark. The difference lies in the effort.

> *I cannot rest from travel; I will drink*
> *Life to the lees.*

In the poem *Ulysses,* Tennyson speaks about the hero who struggled through twenty years of hardship to return to his wife and kingdom. But time has gone by. He is a man of action who now reluctantly governs his people from a civilized throne:

> *How dull it is to pause, to make an end,*
> *To rust unburnish'd, not to shine in use!*

Ulysses has another course in mind:

Tho' much is taken, much abides; and tho'
We are not now that strength which in old days
Moved earth and heaven, that which we are, we are,
One equal temper of heroic hearts,
Made weak by time and fate, but strong in will
To strive, to seek, to find, and not to yield.

In our present state of sleep, we are unable to realize our extraordinary potential. How many of us can claim to "drink life to the lees"? Instead, we are carried along by forces that move us inexorably away from the possibility of consciousness. Unless I am able to develop a finer quality of attention that can, through effort, gradually overcome the compelling forces of sleep, my present efforts will probably amount to little.

But I have a choice. I can continue relying on conditional comforts, secure for the moment, like the deer in the enclosure. Or I can claim my freedom—to shine in use. Freedom is not without risk. Nor is it without effort. It requires a heroic heart. I need to acknowledge my actions and begin to take responsibility for them. To do this, a payment is required. The payment is attention. To gain my freedom, I need to reclaim the keen awareness of the deer at the watering hole. I need to begin to see as if my life depended on it.

last day, last breath

*Recognizing that the **time** we have is **precious**, how can we learn to make the best use of it?*

Time is definitely running out for each of us. It is a simple, inescapable fact. One day will be the last day. One breath will be the last breath. No one has ever escaped this unalterable fate.

The most powerful kings in history are gone. The mightiest generals and their armies are all gone. Those with mountains of wealth have left it all behind. If they had the power, they would still be here. But they are not.

The saints are gone. The great teachers are gone. We would be so fortunate if they could have stayed, but they had to go.

No one lives forever. About seventy years or so is our allotment—a hundred in some rare cases. In the scope of time, life is truly a brief candle.

time is running out

No power on earth can forestall death forever. But deep down inside, most of us reject this idea. We say, "Yes, my time will come, but not yet. Others may have to go, but not me. Not right now." But what guarantee can we claim? Look inside yourself. You may find a furtive idea lurking there. "Although everyone will have to go, I'll somehow be the one to escape. At the very last moment, a miracle will happen or I'll get a reprieve from some governor in the sky. Even though everyone else who has ever lived has had to go before me, still there might be a chance. Perhaps I'll be the single exception in the vast span of human history."

Perhaps. But with those odds, could you find a single sensible person to bet on you?

Time is running out. Because I don't wholeheartedly accept that fact, I have fallen into the habit of putting off until tomorrow all that I could accomplish today. What's the rush, after all? Tomorrow always comes.

But even that is far from certain. There is no assurance that we'll wake up tomorrow morning. No one can guarantee that he or she will be around the next day, much less seventy years from now. You can make a bet based on the averages like an insurance actuary, but that guarantees nothing. Many will go to sleep tonight, never to awaken. The only thing we can be sure of is that one day someone else will be collecting on our life insurance policy.

The bodies we have are extremely fragile. Consider what it takes to reach even the age of early adulthood. Think of all the care that went into preserving your body. You had to feed it and water it every day, keep it warm, treat it with medicines, keep it safe from all sorts of dangers. Yet even the prick of a single thorn can kill it. The bite of a tiny insect can poison it. An infinitesimal microbe can destroy it.

We inhabit a world where it is very difficult to create and very easy to destroy. Think of how much effort went into building your home and acquiring all the possessions in it. Yet the flame from one careless match can reduce it all to ashes.

You might think that if we could preserve the body from all harm, discover a way keep it from aging, and continue to nourish it, we could stay here forever. It seems that medical science is heading in that direction. Perhaps. But the greater problem is that everything changes. The sun that sustains us on this planet will eventually consume its fuel and die. Then let's build an ark and sail to another star, you might say. It's conceivable. You could spend all your time dreaming up novel ways to escape death while inhabiting this body. But all that thinking hasn't added an extra moment to the span of your life. Quite the opposite: From the moment we are born, we are galloping without pause to our demise.

an appointment in Samara

There is a well-known Sufi tale about this headlong dash. Once, a merchant in old Baghdad sent his servant to the marketplace to make arrangements for a feast. A short while later the servant rushed back empty-handed with a look of terror on his face. His master told him to calm himself and explain what was wrong. In the medina, the servant said, he was jostled by a stranger in the crowd. When he turned to scold the rude fellow, he saw to his horror the hooded figure of Death. Before the servant could speak, Death raised his bony hand in a threatening gesture. The servant ran off in fright before Death could grasp him. Now the servant begged his master the loan of a horse. He was going to ride to his relatives in Samara to ask them to hide him from Death. The master gave the terrified servant the horse and watched him gallop off. Later that day the merchant went down to the market where he found Death still among the crowd. "Why did you threaten my servant like that?" the merchant demanded of Death. "I didn't mean to threaten him," Death replied. "I was merely startled to see him here this morning in Baghdad, for I have an appointment with him this evening in Samara."

Is this a dismal prospect? It depends on how you view it. If you are trying desperately to hold onto this life, then you will ultimately face defeat. If, however, you wish to truly appreciate your life, then you must first realize how very precious it is. Right now, you possess something for which a dying king would trade his kingdom. A wealthy person would part with all his wealth to retain it. What else can we human beings find that is so rare and so precious?

death as a reminder of life

Yet we can only begin to appreciate the preciousness of our life when we cease denying its true nature and trying to fool-ishly hold on to it. I don't recommend being careless with it—absolutely not. We all hear stories of ordinary people risking their lives without hesitation to save others. We honor those people as heroes, but not because of their recklessness. Rather, we respect them because they demonstrate by their actions how precious life is. They are willing to risk their own lives to preserve someone else's. It is the recognition of their willingness to sacrifice something so precious that stirs us. By the same token, we are revolted and horrified by the senseless waste of life we see every day in the news. We recognize that something of irreplaceable value has been squandered.

Yet we have a strange way of looking at our own lives. Most of us act as if we are going to live forever. But the only way we can really appreciate life is by paying attention to it. We need a compelling enough reason to make the effort to develop attention. Otherwise, our attention wanders here and there, caught up in the fascinating glitter of the marketplace. Then we catch a glimpse of Death in the crowd and we bolt in fear.

The trick is not to cower from death, but to learn to appreciate life—how wonderful it is, how full of potential. But also how brief. Death should serve as a reminder. Recognizing and keeping in mind that death is inevitable will help us appreciate life. If we can do that, it will lead us to become more mindful about how we live.

the forest
and the trees

chapter 3

*Mindfulness means both **awareness***

*of ourselves in the **present** moment*

*and an **appreciation** of our **connection***

to the rest of life, giving rise to a need

for thoughtful, careful attention.

I am walking through the woods on a gray day at the very end of autumn. The smell of snow is in the air. All of the leaves have fallen except those of the rustling red oaks, which will hang on through the winter. The last of the geese have flown by, honking in their V-formations, heading south ahead of the snow. I'm by the edge of the beaver pond, looking at the tall pines across the water and worrying about whether I'll be able to renew the mortgage that comes due in five years. Will I have enough in the bank? Can I generate enough income? Will I have to sell and move on? Just then, the first flurries of the season begin to gently fall. I find myself standing there, not begging at some banker's desk five years hence, but standing in the woods watching the first signs of winter. I can feel my feet on the ground and, with that, I begin to get a glimmer of my place in the world. I am not only standing in the woods at the edge of a pond but I am also moving in the stream of life.

If I am fortunate enough, I may achieve a moment when I finally realize that, like the deer at the watering hole, I am indeed here and alive in the world. For a moment, I may feel grateful to be alive. I realize how much of life is lived without being present in the here and now.

Not only are my feet on the ground, but the ground is part of the planet. The planet has other people in it—people just like me with the same needs and desires. We are moving together in this stream. Each of us affects the other. I am intimately connected with these people and depend on their kindness for my very life. Can I begin to see that because I am intimately connected, my actions have consequences? Can I begin to act mindfully, aware of my own ripples in this river of life?

Some independent-minded persons might object to the notion that their very lives depend on the kindness of others. After all, it is possible to raise your own food, sew your own clothes, build your own shelter, and live apart from every other human being.

For the moment that might be true, but was it always so? There was a time in the life of every human being when he or she was totally dependent on the kindness and care of others. There was a time when you couldn't walk, speak, or even feed yourself. Yet day after day someone cared for you and kept you alive.

The day arrived when you could wander off, if you so chose, to become a hermit in the woods, claiming total independence from others. But before that day, when you were helpless, what would have happened if the person caring for you thoughtlessly forgot to feed you, carelessly neglected to keep you warm, mindlessly let you tumble to the ground? How would you have survived to claim your independence from others? It would have been impossible.

We may find fault with those who have cared for us, but the simple fact remains that if someone had not fed and clothed us and protected us from a thousand daily harms, we would not be here today.

Without a doubt, we need to develop the kind of attention that enables us to become aware of ourselves. But that awareness must expand to encompass the sense of our place in the world and our interconnectedness to it. We need to see both forest and trees. Without that broader awareness, it is difficult to develop a real appreciation of the consequences of our actions. Without that more expansive understanding, we stand a first-rate chance of sowing more suffering.

Can anyone really be content while those around them are suffering? I'm not speaking about the nameless, faceless poor on a distant continent. I'm speaking about your spouse, your children, your friends, and your family. If your actions are contributing to their unhappiness, how much contentment will you be able to find? Sooner or later, they'll complain or leave, or at the least you'll be greeted by their miserable expressions at the dinner table. You might be able to wolf down your meal under those unhappy conditions, but how satisfying will it be?

the importance of skillfulness

Consider for a moment the opposite of mindfulness. What sort of behavior does that engender? What is the result of careless, thoughtless actions other than to cause suffering?

By making an inattentive mistake while keeping the bees, both they and I suffered. Opening the hive on a deceptively balmy autumn day, I was stung and bees died needlessly. It was not a wanton or willful act on my part. But my lack of awareness of the larger picture led to carelessness. And suffering was the result. None of us in our right minds wishes to cause suffering. Yet we do.

We need to acquire skillfulness in navigating through this life. This is the real import of mindfulness. We can see the consequences of thoughtless action every day. I'm sorry to say the news reeks of it. On every scale, mindless activity is creating new troubles for us. Children suffer from broken homes. Parents suffer when their children go astray. The elderly suffer neglect. The poor struggle to make their way. Those with jobs worry about keeping them. Those better off worry about preserving their assets, as white-collar criminals undermine our economy. Terrorism has people everywhere living in fear for their lives.

You might say, "These problems have always plagued human beings. I'm just trying to make my own life a little more peaceful and balanced. What can I, by myself, do about all these issues? Shouldn't I just try to tend my own backyard?"

Yes, certainly. In fact, where else could you begin? But your backyard borders on someone else's. When I moved to the country some years ago, I was represented by an elderly lawyer who had been the town's mayor for more than forty years. By his demeanor, it was clear he had seen it all. There was a wood with nothing but a little shack on it across the road from my new property. The road was little traveled.

The shack itself was not visible from my place. I was told the people who owned it used it only a few times a year. Nevertheless, envisioning bulldozers toppling the trees and homes being built up and down the road, I asked the lawyer to look into who owned the wood and shack and whether they might be interested in selling. The lawyer agreed to take on this new assignment if I really wanted him to. He paused a moment to let me reflect on this. Then he said, "Yes, I can look into it. But where are you going to stop?"

Now I can see the other side of his question. Where are you going to start? If I want to live in a better, more peaceful world, it's up to me to do something about it, beginning in my own backyard.

Ram Dass, the former Richard Alpert, traveled to India where he met Maharaj-ji, who became his teacher. Ram Dass was deeply impressed by his first encounter, feeling that Maharaj-ji looked into his heart and saw everything there was to see. After some time, Ram Dass finally had a moment alone with his guru. He asked Maharaj-ji the question that had brought him to India in the first place: "How do I become enlightened?" Maharaj-ji simply answered, "Help people, feed people." To me, Maharaj-ji's words read like a prescription for mindfulness.

But remember that you, yourself, are also one of those people. To help others, you have to begin with helping yourself. To help rather than harm, we need to develop mindfulness.

touched to
the heart

chapter 4

Many cultures locate the mind at the

__heart__ center. When we open our __minds__

to a real sense of our interconnectedness,

we find our hearts open as well.

Imagine for a moment that you want to emphatically declare your intentions. If someone is asking for your assent, you may vigorously nod your head. If someone is calling for a volunteer, you may raise your hand. But suppose someone is asking who is next in a long line at the ticket counter? Who is the owner of this sack of gold bullion? Who is fairest of them all? "It's me," you say as you point determinedly to yourself. If you're like me, you'll find yourself pointing your finger at the center of your chest.

Traditional cultures call this place the heart center. In the East, it is known as the heart *chakra*—the real seat of the mind, rather than the head, where we in the West point when indicating the location of our thoughts. As citizens of the West, we may find that we spend most of our time rummaging around in that attic we call the brain, sorting through dusty recollections of the past or anxious dreamy thoughts of the future.

In the narrow attic of conventional thought, I am blocked from the expansiveness of the heart. As I am now, habits and tensions cut me off from my feelings. The way is blocked by a kind of grasping that arises from a confused view of what is essential. This grasping is subtle but pervasive.

I am grasping at what I think will make me happy. I am grasping at what I think will sustain me in this body. I am grasping at my own identity. I am grasping because I fear I will lose everything I need and desire if I don't hold tightly to it. This underlying fear of loss constrains me in countless ways. The positive qualities of generosity, discipline, patience, enthusiasm, and concentration are all weakened and under-mined by this grasping. Most sadly of all, this fearful tension prevents my heart from opening. We can only truly be touched when we are open. Otherwise we hide inside a guarded wall of tension, fending off an army of imagined threats. This is no way to live.

I need to use mindfulness to forge a path back to my heart. When the mind, body, and feelings are connected, a new view is possible. But our unconscious tensions block these connections and throw things out of balance. The tensions restrict the flow of energy through the body. The restricted flow of energy causes imbalances in the body's four elements, traditionally described in the East as earth, air, fire, and water. When these elements are out of balance, we become tired, weak, ill.

dealing with bad habits

Even from a conventional Western viewpoint, we can see that each of these unconscious tensions consumes energy. These tensions become habits that are sustained through a lack of awareness. I clench my jaw in anxiety until my teeth hurt. I grip a pencil as if it weighs a hundred pounds. I tap my foot in impatience waiting for the train until my ankle aches. I crane my neck as I sit at the keyboard, anxious to finish my work. All these unconscious tensions waste energy that I could better apply to consciousness. We already have seen that our time in this body is limited. The energy available to us in our present state is also limited. And with every unconscious habit, it is draining away. Now is a good time to stop the leaks.

It seems a strange quirk of the language, but attention eliminates tension. Look at yourself right now:

* *First, look for the tensions in your posture. You may be clenching your jaw. You may be sitting with one foot cocked under the other. Observe the tension this is producing. Train your attention on this tension.*

* *Breathe. Keep your awareness on the tension. See how it begins to relax. If it is a long-standing habit, the tension will probably return as your attention wanders.*

* *But then something calls you back to yourself and your intention. You become aware once more of the habit of clenching your jaw or hunching your shoulders and you begin to relax again.*

The habits of posture can only operate in the darkness outside your attention. Illuminate them with awareness and they begin to fade.

We can turn this kind of attention on our habitual views as well. I said earlier that when I come to a sense of myself here and now, my view of my interdependence in the world begins to open. Generally my view of my interconnectedness to life is blocked and constrained by grasping. In order to reduce this grasping, I need to open my mind to my place in the world around me. By opening my mind, I can open my heart.

How do I go about opening my mind? By patiently presenting it with the truth. That is the work of mindfulness—to slowly, patiently begin to see things as they are. It is my confused view of the nature of my life that gives rise to my tense and fearful grasping. This view makes me think that I am the most important one, the only one. If I don't grab what I need right now and defend it against all competitors, I will be out of luck. In a dog-eat-dog world, that may be true. But even dogs don't often eat each other. In fact they do a pretty good job of caring for their young, protecting the members of their pack, and working together to procure food. In fact, once a dog accepts you as his friend, he will lay down his life defending you.

Each and every one of us is alive because of the kindness of others. Few of us these days grows all his or her own food, fashions all his or her own clothes, forges all his or her own tools, or builds his or her own shelter. In countless ways, we depend on the hard work and the good efforts of each other. Even in these troubled times, you can see that a vast number of people are looking out for each other. If we all acted in what we imagine is a dog-eat-dog manner, there would be no teachers to teach our young. There would be no one to nurse us through illness. There would be no one to protect us from danger. There would be no one to save us from fire, flood, and famine. We hear about such generous acts every day. Whether we recognize it or not, all of us have always relied on the kindness of strangers.

We need to open our minds by patiently convincing ourselves of the folly of thinking only of ourselves and ignoring the needs of others. One Tibetan verse tries to convince us of this by making a striking comparison and asking us to reflect on it.

> *In short, the naive work for their aims alone,*
> *While Buddhas work solely to benefit others.*
> *Comparing my efforts to theirs, who is better off?*
> *Inspire me to be able to exchange self-interest*
>   *for interest in the welfare of others.*

If you want to be free, look to those who have achieved freedom in their lives. What method did they follow? If you look around the world today, you may not be able to find Buddhas at work on every corner. But we can take inspiration from the more open-hearted actually among us, those who have decided to make their lives be of some benefit to others. Compare their lives with those who appear to be working solely for their own self-interest and decide who is better off.

paying
attention

chapter 5

In the beginning, we need a reliable

motivation *to carry out the effort*

of awareness. Without a strong sense

*of **purpose**, we are unlikely to make*

the required effort.

Seeing that the chronic disease of self-cherishing
Is the cause of my unwanted suffering,
Inspire me to put the blame where blame is due
And vanquish the great demon of clinging to self.

FROM THE TIBETAN *OFFERING TO THE SPIRITUAL GUIDE*

Selfishness is the culprit that steals our happiness. This thief can be pursued only through mindfulness. The wise recognize this and cultivate a generous heart that overcomes this clinging demon. Hardhearted people may scoff at the notion of generosity as a form of weakness. After all, this is a tough world. If you hope to survive you had better look out for yourself first. Let's be generous and call their argument practical. But weren't these same practical persons helpless once—as infants wholly dependent on the generosity of others? Even in the cruelest environments, there was some shred of human kindness. Somehow they were fed and looked after. Let's say for a moment that they did endure a cruel and harsh childhood. What made it harsh? The selfish, thoughtless, mindless actions of others. What would have made it a kind and gentle place? Only the thoughtful care and concern of others. This gentle place arises through mindful action.

We create our own environment, whether it's cruel or kind. We see this on every scale. We create unhappy households through our thoughtless actions. We pollute the air we breathe and the water we drink through selfish shortsightedness. Mahatma Gandhi, speaking of the strife in the world, said the earth is capable of supplying everyone's need, but it could never satisfy even a single person's greed. Selfish action can never produce happiness. It may bring mountains of material satisfaction. But that satisfaction is bound to be temporary if it is based on greed because greed can never be satisfied. Once you become its slave, greed will drive you mercilessly to fulfill its bottomless desires.

Are we under any obligation to act mindfully? It all depends on how you view the consequences of all of your actions. If you think selfish actions will bring you happiness, you will doubtlessly pursue that path. Many have gone before you. How did it turn out for them? Ask their squabbling heirs.

treat life as a precious gift

In the end, it is a matter of choice. How do you want to spend your life? It's your time to spend as you wish. I believe we are far better off if we treat life as the precious gift that it really is. But it's a gift we will ultimately have to relinquish. Grasping it like a miser while we are alive will not help us develop real appreciation for it. In order to know how to spend it wisely we need to develop mindfulness.

The wise urge us to adopt a more expansive view. They recognize that, in the end, we breathe the same air. We drink from the same well. In the case of enlightened beings, love and compassion are said to be both boundless and effortless. Like us, these enlightened people were motivated by a desire for happiness and freedom from suffering. The difference is that their wish for happiness and freedom from suffering includes everyone.

We can get a glimpse of this kind of love and compassion if we consider a loving mother. How could she possibly be happy knowing her child was suffering? Wouldn't she do all in her power to free her child from suffering, never resting until her child was safe and happy? Wouldn't she act with the strongest possible motivation to bring this about, putting all concern for herself aside? Wouldn't she give her life without hesitation to save her child from harm? Such a mother provides a strong example of actions born out of love (the desire to see her child happy) and compassion (the wish to free her child from suffering).

A loving mother may be able to extend this mindful care to her child—alert and attentive to its every need. But she may not be able to provide this kind of care to every child in the world. Although a loving mother reacts to her own child's need, enlightened beings act with utmost mindfulness to bring happiness and freedom from suffering to all beings.

It's safe to say most of our lives are a far cry from that. In fact, enlightenment may not be your goal at all. You may wish for a calmer, more collected life. You may hope for some peace of mind. You may want a keener sense of this life, here and now, with all it has to offer. You may want to become a better person, kinder and more open and generous to those around you, and you believe cultivating mindfulness may be of some help. Who could argue with that? Whatever your goal, you need a proper motivation in order to attain it. Otherwise, why would you act?

valuing mindfulness

This is not surprising. Every action we take is propelled by some kind of motivation. To begin and sustain the work required for developing mindfulness, we need solid and reliable motivation. Can we see how acting thoughtlessly and mindlessly brings about suffering for ourselves and others? Can we see how mindfulness can lead to freedom from this kind of suffering? Can we see how living mindfully can help us make the best use of this precious life? If we can, then we will begin to value mindfulness. If we value it, we will be willing to make the effort required to cultivate it.

If I can consider the needs of all other beings as my motivation for acting mindfully, that's wonderful. But that might be a tall order at the present time. If I can see how acting mindfully will be of benefit for myself that is enough to begin making an effort.

As human beings we also have another quirk we need to take into account. The truth is that we really value only what we pay for. We may cling to possessions given to us, but we don't really value them. To understand what something is worth, it seems we have to pay for it with our own efforts. We pay for mindfulness with attention.

Attention has great power to overcome tensions, habits, and the negative emotions that give rise to suffering. The payment of attention brings its own reward. But right now, for most of us, it is in short supply.

Try following the second hand on your watch. See if you can concentrate on it for sixty seconds, paying attention only to your breath, without your focus wavering. Try to be honest with yourself for an entire minute. If you're like me, you'll soon sense the rising tide of distractions.

What else do I need to do today? Is that a car pulling into the drive? Is it too cool in here? Why am I sitting here staring at my watch? Do I really have so little attention? Thoughts begin to seep in, ready to capture my attention and carry me off.

But what else do I have to pay with besides attention? Without it, I will continue to act thoughtlessly. With it, I begin to act with all the care and attentiveness that this precious life deserves.

When we see how difficult it is to actually pay attention, we begin to appreciate the effort required to develop it. I won't achieve the boundless awareness of enlightenment by focusing on my watch for sixty seconds. I can't expect to see the broad expanse of life in one fell swoop. But by making small repeated payments, I can begin to strengthen my power of concentration. I need this concentration because there is a thief lurking close by, waiting to take advantage of my lapsing attention.

glimpsing
the thief

chapter 6

*Our joy and **appreciation** of our lives*

are robbed by our negative qualities, which

lead us to suffering again and again.

*To **free** ourselves from the grip of these*

qualities, so that we can benefit ourselves

*and others, we need to develop **attention**.*

There is a thief who has followed me my whole life. I have rarely seen him though I have never been far from him. He haunts me like a shadow. If I ride out into the middle of a wide, open plain and sit contentedly under the empty sky, he still sneaks up from behind. The moment my back is turned, he slips in and snatches my contentment. The thief wears the negative guises of attachment, anger, and ignorance.

I'm reasonably sure he's after you, too. Few of us are completely free from his depredations. He arises from a basic misunderstanding of our nature. It is a misunderstanding so basic and pervasive we barely see it. When I feel someone has wronged me, I may get a glimpse of it. If I believe I am falsely accused, something in me immediately rises to the defense. "How dare you?" it says. I feel this solid sense of "me" hotly rising to the occasion. This strident fellow is the one I'm after.

Most of us will jump from blame as if it were a snake about to strike. We will immediately point a finger at someone or something else. You might say we do it because we fear punishment. I think it goes deeper than that. We're defending our identity. We spend our days and nights serving and protecting this identity. It seems so solid, yet we react as if it were the most fragile thing in the world. It is sensitive to the merest slight. Something as intangible as a wayward look from a stranger on the street is enough to send it into a tailspin.

Imagine for a moment that you have tried to slight the Buddha. How much of a rise do you suppose you'd get from him? Contrast that with our own capacity for perceiving insult. Even our politeness is usually not much more than a masquerade that covers a nearly comical degree of touchiness. If we could see ourselves engaging in our polite parries and feints all day long, like a drunken musketeer, we would have to laugh. We are merely defending our honor, we say. No one should slavishly bear wrongs, we might argue. Fine. But first determine who or what is being wronged. Then see what role slavishness plays.

This thief appears as ignorance, attachment, and anger. The first is ignorance, this misapprehension about our identity that makes most of us so excruciatingly defensive. We are thoroughly convinced there is something to defend. We fully believe that our identity is threatened by insults and accusations. We react with blinding speed when we feel it is being attacked. I am not speaking about threats to our health or well-being that put our lives in danger. We should try to preserve this precious life and not needlessly throw it away. I am speaking about insults to this imperious little tyrant called the ego. He is the one who has enslaved me. The one who steals all my joy. The one whose unrelenting demands wear me down. He wants to become solid. He wants to live forever. He counters every threat to his existence with sound and fury. "Pay no attention to that fellow behind the curtain," he says. "I am the great and powerful Oz." Humbug.

If he is so great and powerful, then why don't we enjoy perfect freedom and happiness right now? Why do we fall prey to illness? Why do we have to work and struggle to feed ourselves? We all strive for happiness, yet this fellow leads us into the soup nearly every time. Listen to him make excuses, shifting the blame and defending his weakness and failure to produce happiness with a litany of "If only." If only so–and–so would do my bidding. If only such–and–such were out of my way. If only those fools would recognize my great talent, contributions, holiness, intelligence, humility, award-winning smile—you name it.

The point is, this fellow can never lead us to happiness. He is far too busy propping up his dictatorship to lead us anywhere but into trouble. Instead we are fed a steady diet of propaganda to make us believe that without him we are nothing. Without him, we would have no identity. He makes us afraid that we will lose ourselves if we let go of him for a split second. We have been ruled by this belief our entire lives.

A renowned Tibetan meditator was once asked to describe his method. The questioner expected to learn about some esoteric practice. Instead he said,

I stand guard at the entrance to my cave with a sword in hand. When the thief appears, I strike him without hesitation.

Up to now we have welcomed this thief with an open door. We have served him at our table again and again. And each time he has made off with our joy, our happiness, our peace of mind. We struggle so hard to acquire these qualities and, in a moment, this thief snatches them.

To catch this thief and send him packing, we first need to recognize him for what he is the moment he shows his face. To maintain vigilance, we need to understand the worth of what is being stolen from us. To vanquish this criminal once and for all, we need to develop awareness.

This thieving tyrant called ignorance is kept in power by two henchmen, the negative qualities of anger and attachment. They harry us in ways great and small, stealing our contentment and engaging us in the kind of strife that distracts us from the true source of the trouble.

Let's have a look at this attachment fellow first. The Buddha taught that its basis is craving and I think the word is apt. We want things. When we don't get them we are unhappy. I once spent some time riding around in the company of a police detective. He was going through the inventory of crimes available to the human species. He noted that even the worst crimes fell into one of two categories. They were motivated either by love or money. In modern times we equate money with power, but when you leaf through Shakespeare you'll find the same catalog of motivations. Shakespeare's characters desire something and their failure to possess it undoes them. Othello's foolish belief that Desdemona is possessed by another does them both in. Macbeth craves kingship and watches in horror when Birnam Wood comes marching to Dunsinane. Brutus wants to remain righteous in the hearts and minds of Romans and is persuaded through his high-mindedness to slay Caesar.

We, too, are immersed in daily little dramas. We may not play such Shakespearean roles, but we are fueled by similar desires and frustrations. We don't get what we want and the tyrannical ego boils over with anger. As a result, this anger—born of these frustrated desires—simmers up all over town.

We feel insulted, hurt, outraged. Shouts and imprecations fill the air. Just another day's work for anger and attachment, as the dictator sinks more deeply into his seat of power.

If you longed for freedom in a country controlled by a despot, you might make plans to escape. If your loved ones lived there too, you'd try to help them escape with you. If that wasn't possible, then you might realize that you had to overthrow the tyrant to win your freedom.

This tyrant ego is the true target of mindfulness. As with any campaign, we need to develop a workable strategy. We need to marshal and train our forces. We need to plan and build our resources so we can sustain ourselves for the long struggle. We need courage and resolve. We need the determination that comes from knowing our cause is just.

Know from the beginning that the one thing this fellow cannot stand is the direct light of attention. It may be very difficult to catch even a glimpse of him and his machinations at first. But if we continue to practice, if we patiently observe our actions without instantly reacting to them, we will begin to see his stealthy hand at work. We will become more and more like the monk guarding the entrance to his cave with his swift, shining sword—ready to challenge the thief.

can you get there from here?

chapter 7

Businesspeople use the term return on investment *to decide whether it's worth going ahead with a project. Since developing mindfulness requires* **effort** *as well as our precious* **time**, *we should know what we hope to* **achieve**, *how we intend to achieve it, and whether we are* **investing** *in a reliable method.*

Our time is precious. Most of us would like to profit from it rather than see it wasted. But life is a risky business. Depending on your nature, you can gamble or try to invest where there is a reasonable chance of return.

Deciding to practice mindfulness is no different than making other investments. If you were investing in a business, you would want to examine its business plan. The plan would present a view of the market, identify a need for that market, and explain how the business would go about successfully filling that need. There would be a budget explaining how capital would be raised and spent in the time it would take to realize a profit. You'd look over these details and decide whether this venture stood a reasonable chance of success before you committed yourself. There are no guarantees, but a thoughtful examination of the facts would allow you to make an informed decision.

The Buddha urged his students 2,500 years ago to make the same critical evaluation of his teachings. He told them not to take his words at face value but to treat them as if they were a piece of gold being considered for purchase. If you were buying gold, you'd subject it to every test you could think of to determine its purity. In the same way, the Buddha asked his disciples to test the truth of his teachings for themselves.

We engage in reckless ventures all the time, often without recognizing the risks. We act on hearsay, or intuition, or a cast of the dice and hope for the best. However we choose to act, we do it with the faith that our choice is for the best. But it would be better if we acted with intelligence rather than with blind faith. Blind faith offers the same assurances as wild gambling. It can lead to riches once in a blue moon, but it more often ends in bankruptcy. In more tragic instances, blind faith is quite capable of leading you over the cliff thinking it's a path to freedom. These are often the unhappy consequences of fanaticism.

choosing a suitable path

As human beings, we all have the advantage of an intelligent, discerning mind. We should use it to examine the truth of what we find, and determine whether it provides a suitable path for us. We won't be able to know all the facts and their long-range consequences in perfect detail, but we can determine whether the path we are pursuing has proven reliable in the past. We can decide if it tallies with our own observations and experience. We have the great tool of basic common sense. Ask yourself:

- *Does the path you are interested in pursing make sense?*

- *Does it offer steps that you can reasonably hope to follow through your own efforts?*

- *Does one step lead to the next to get you where you wish to go?*

Traditional Tibetan teachings will tell you to examine three points when choosing to follow a path. These aspects are called *base*, *method*, and *result*:

- **Base** *is what you are working with. In the case of mindfulness, we are working with the mind.*

- *The* **method** *we are using is the development of attention through patient, steady practice.*

- *The* **result** *we are aiming at is a more stabilized, expansive mind that is capable of focusing on the work at hand. With this attention, we can begin to dismantle once and for all the vast array of delusions that hide the truth from us.*

As Jesus said:
And you shall know the truth,
*   and the truth shall make you free.*

But to know the truth, we have to be able to see it. That requires training our minds to be capable of real discernment.

taming the wild horse

We are trying to tame the wild horse of the mind and make it work for us. It may be capable of swift and powerful feats, but we are incapable of reining it in just yet.

I kept horses for a number of years out in the country. Sitting here now, it occurs to me that this activity is not much different from mindful practice. You're faced with a frisky young horse. You'd like to be able to ride it some day on the trails over the hills to watch the quiet sunset. You're willing to feed the colt and care for it with every consideration for its health and well-being, but you also need to tame it. This can be done roughly or thoughtfully. People often speak of *breaking a horse,* and I've seen it done. I'd rather let horses run wild, if that were the only way to achieve the goal. But it is not.

If you observe carefully, you'll see that the horse is quite willing to learn. But you first have to take into account its attention span. In the beginning, it quickly grows tired of learning. You need to be aware of this and not push too hard.

You also need to be aware of the conditions where the learning takes place. Horses are creatures of habit—a new sight can rattle and distract them. You need to be aware of this and not think the horse has suddenly become stubborn or flighty for no reason. Your own relationship to the horse— where you stand, how you move, what you say—is sensitively perceived by the horse. In fact, a horse provides a keen reflection of your own state once you begin to observe its reactions.

If you work patiently, after a time you will begin to see results. Soon, it will become quite clear that the horse is enjoying the work. It will come to meet you at the gate.

It may even nuzzle you for its halter, knowing it means new adventures outside the confines of the corral.

You are willing to take the time to patiently perform these tasks because you have learned from others that they lead to results and because you see for yourself that they make sense. They take into account both the nature of the horse and the nature of the rider. If followed with diligence and care, they will produce the results you desire. Your time will not have been spent in vain. One fine evening, you'll find yourself up on the ridge looking at the rosy clouds to the west. Both of you—horse and rider—will be there at sunset, quiet, at peace, almost as if you were one.

part two

MIND

DEVELOPING
ULNESS
developing mindfulness

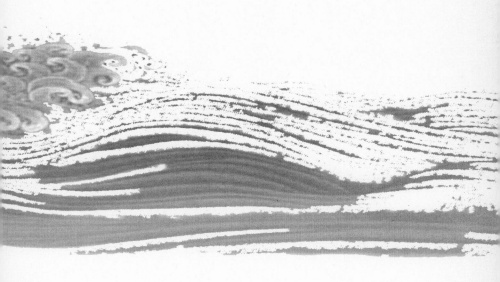

eh?
hmm...ah!

chapter 8

*The realization of any practice involves **learning** about it, **analyzing** it, and finally "**getting**" it, so it becomes an integral part of your experience.*

Archimedes, the Greek philosopher, was sitting in his bathtub a couple of thousand years ago. He had been pondering the question of how to know for certain if a king's crown was pure gold or some baser alloy being passed off as gold. Archimedes knew from his study of nature that equal volumes of different alloys have different weights. Given two rings of the same size, one of gold and the other of silver, the gold ring will tilt the balance in its favor. If he could find a means to compare the weight of the crown with an equal volume of gold, he could determine if the crown was pure. He could balance the crown against a block of gold on a scale readily enough. But how could he know if they were the same volume? The volume of the block of gold was easy to calculate, but the shape of the crown made it difficult to measure. He couldn't very well melt the crown into a lump in order to compare it or the king would have his head. He would have to find another way.

As Archimedes lowered himself into his bathtub, he noticed that the water rose and ran over the rim. "Eureka!" was his famous cry. "I have found it." Legend has it he ran naked through the streets in his elation at his realization. He had saved the crown and his head. What he realized was that equal volumes displace equal amounts of water. If the crown, with its complex shape, and an equal weight of a simple block of gold made the water rise by an equal amount, then they were the same volume. Two metals of equal weight and equal volume could be assumed to be the same material.

Most of us faced with a vexing question know that sense of elation that arises when we finally "get" something. We arrive at something more than simple comprehension. With that "Eureka!" what we have understood becomes an integral part of our experience—a part of ourselves, really.

the three levels of learning

Traditional Tibetan teachings will tell you that to undertake a path, you need to apply three levels of learning to each step in order to make progress. Those levels could be called *learning*, *analyzing*, and *experiencing*.

First, at the learning level, you read or hear about an idea. If it remains at this level, it is merely information. You can memorize volumes and recite them chapter and verse, but without subjecting what you have learned to analysis, you will not have accomplished much more than a parrot.

Archimedes knew that different metals have different weights. If he stopped at the level of simple observation, there wouldn't have been much to shout about. Instead, he thought about this bit of information. He tried to see how it fit with the rest of his knowledge of the world. He wondered what implications arose from it.

The second level, then, is to think about what you have learned. The traditional teachings divide meditation into two types: concentrated meditation and analytical meditation, sometimes referred to as *shamata* and *vipassana*. Both are absolutely necessary to make progress on the path.

Considering what you have learned and looking deeply into it is analytical meditation. You don't need to sit on a cushion to do this work. You may be waiting in a line at the supermarket, riding the train to work, or even sitting in your bathtub. The point is to apply your mind to what you have learned:

- *Analyze it*
- *Question it*
- *Test it*
- *Turn it over in your mind*
- *See if makes sense.*

Once you have examined the point in question, you can practice concentrated meditation. Turn your attention to the point and focus on it in quiet circumstances. Hold it in your mind. Concentrate without distraction on this one point. Of course your attention will waver, but simply recognize this wavering without recrimination and return again to the question. Practice at this level a little each day until your mind grows more accustomed to the work. Sooner or later, like Archimedes, you will see the truth of what you are considering, your own "eureka." It will become part of you. This is the third level of learning—the level of experience. This kind of realization is at the heart of any true practice. This is the real measure of progress.

mindfulness
at mealtimes

We hear an idea that sounds like it might contain some truth. We consider it, turn it over in our minds, see if it tallies with our experience. We come to a point of understanding and focus on it, letting it become more than a thought, until we gain some experience of the truth of it.

You could look at your next meal in this way. You have heard the idea that perhaps you are more dependent on others than you might have thought. If you can recognize the truth of this, you may be able to expand your view to a less self-centered one of yourself.

If you take the source of your meal into account and think about it and the implications—beyond agriculture and economics—for what it tells you about your place in this life, it may help open your mind to a clearer vision of the truth. You may begin to see that we share something and that we depend on each other. You may find your appreciation for what you actually have has increased.

As I sit at the table, I consider how many people contributed to getting the food onto my plate. I just finished a lunch of smoked salmon, goat cheese, capers, and bread. Just think of the ingredients in the bread alone.

- I don't grow wheat

- I don't harvest salt

- I don't make butter

- I don't raise yeast

- I didn't provide the fuel or build the oven to bake it

All these things were provided by the efforts of others. They worked to grow, harvest, refine, and deliver these ingredients, which would take me enormous effort to provide for myself.

I don't even know what a caper is, much less how to find one. Yet I was able to take a break from my work and prepare a simple, satisfying lunch in a few minutes, thanks to the efforts of so many others.

With this in mind, perhaps you will be able to practice a little more mindfulness the next time you sit down to a meal. Who knows? You might taste something new.

grass
in the wind

chapter 9

In our current state, our attention is easily

*distracted by the rush of **outer** activity and*

*the whirl of **inner** thoughts. We need to*

*develop a supple **awareness** that perceives*

*reality from a place of **stillness**.*

I forget myself all the time. I wish to remember that I am here. I want to remain in the present but, despite my intention, I am carried off by every little breeze of distraction. What is it I am trying to remember? I want to take stock of my situation. Not to judge it or comment on it or criticize it, but simply to observe how I am in the moment. I am not trying to change anything. I am only trying to observe myself. What is calling my attention? What is my state? Where are my tensions? I can become engrossed in the task at hand and the hours will fly by. I need to keep my attention on my work, certainly. I also need to reserve something for myself. But I am always getting carried away by the work.

I race sailboats once a week during the summer. The races take place in New York Harbor just before sunset. Often a golden light will wash the skyline of the city and make it seem a place free of trouble. The sounds of the city are replaced by the rush of the wind and the splash of the hull through the water. There is the fresh smell of salt spray and the sensation of the heady gallop of the boat through the waves. The races are fairly competitive and sailing well requires a lot of attention. I have been trying for years to remain fully in the race, yet still enjoy the sights and sounds at sunset. But I could count on the fingers of one hand the times when I have achieved both.

I seem engrossed in what I am doing but my activity rarely gets my full attention. It's a question of balance. I may win the race but I miss the sunset. It's like that with most tasks because my full attention is rarely available to me. How many times have I hammered a nail while thinking about what's for supper? How many meals have I eaten but barely tasted while thinking about shingling the roof?

Knowing how hard it is to remember to focus, I need to take measures to remind me of my intention. I need an "alarm clock" I can depend on to remind me of what I am trying to achieve. So I choose something outside myself that will call me back when I have forgotten. I could tell myself things like:

- *Each time I call for a course change, I will breathe in sights and sounds of the harbor.*

- *Each time I pick up a nail, I will feel the weight of the hammer in my hand.*

- *Each time I walk through a doorway, I will remember to sense my feet on the floor.*

- *Each time I lift a fork, I will consider where my meal came from.*

Then I can check myself at the end of the day to see how often I remembered. Not with recrimination but observation. For now, that is enough.

I am trying to develop attention. I am looking for the source of my distractions. I want to train my attention on that source each time I see it. I am not trying to change anything. That would get in the way of seeing what I need to see. What is drawing me away from myself? What are the thoughts that carry me off? Seeing this will begin to give me a picture of the identity I have constructed for myself. It is an identity that is defined by countless attractions and aversions. I am so enrapt in them that I can barely see them. My reactions are so swift and compelling that I am hardly aware that they are taking place.

I walk down a city street. My eye is caught by a display of high-tech gadgets in a shop window. I gaze sideways at the gizmos, no longer seeing the path ahead. A couple of raffish fellows are leaning in the doorway, so I put on my stone-faced city glare to ward off trouble. An attractive woman is heading my way, so I straighten my shoulders and puff out my chest. Someone steps in my way without looking, so my face takes on a frown of indignation. I tap my foot against the curb with impatience, waiting for the light to change. Why should I, with a host of important business transactions before me, be forced to wait along with this mob? A chauffered private car rolls by and I peer at its occupants wondering how they acquired the means for such obvious luxury. It goes on like this all the way across town, until I remember why I am here.

Can I witness my reactions even as they are taking place? Can I get a feeling for what lies behind each distraction? Instead of being carried off by it, can I watch this whirl from a place of stillness?

watching the whirl

We are engaged in countless activities throughout the day. Each one of them is an opportunity for mindfulness—if we can remember our intention. As we are now, we are quite likely to forget as we become involved in the busy routines of our lives. If we can find a way to remind ourselves, we can take advantage of these routines to look more deeply into ourselves.

As you set out in your day, try looking ahead to activities that you will perform:

- *Taking a phone call*

- *Waiting in line for the bus*

- *Walking into work*

- *Opening and closing the door*

- *Sitting down at your desk*

- *Eating your lunch.*

You can choose one of those events to serve as a reminder.

For example, you can tell yourself that you will look at your state each time the telephone rings.

- Where was I when the phone rang?

- Was I aware of myself or a million miles away?

- How am I sitting? Am I relaxed or cramped in some unconscious tension?

- How am I reacting to the telephone's ring?

- Am I anticipating the call or wishing to avoid it?

- Am I resentful of the intrusion or welcoming the distraction?

Try to see how each of these reactions is colored by desire or aversion. Try to get a sense of how much of your sense of yourself is made up of these subtle likes and dislikes. See if you can glimpse the shadow of the thief.

center
of gravity

chapter 10

*Mindfulness helps **steady**, **stabilize**, and*

***strengthen** the power of our attention and*

*increases our **"center of gravity"** so we*

become less easily swayed by distraction.

When I have the opportunity, I like to wander through the Asian wing of the Metropolitan Museum of Art in New York. This section has many statues of Buddhas. The figures of these enlightened beings are from different areas in the East and were made in different centuries. In figure after figure, regardless of its provenance, I find the same quality. I call it a *center of gravity*. When I regard these figures, I find it impossible to imagine their being swayed by anything. They are in perfect repose, yet they are fully aware. They are without fear and without surprise. I can imagine nothing that could disturb them.

What I am seeing is stillness. These figures are telling me about a possibility within myself—the possibility of silence. As I am now, I am easily swayed by outer distractions and inner thoughts. Either can pull my attention in its direction. I lack a center of gravity. Yet these seated figures hold out the possibility of developing this center. They remain aware but unswayed by outer and inner distractions.

The forces that keep us lurching this way and that are the same old swindlers—fear, desire, and aversion. They continue to prop up the ego by stealing our attention. As long as we are prey to these distractions, we are unable to accumulate the kind of attention that will tilt the balance in our favor.

The figures of the enlightened beings in the museum represent those who have freed themselves from these thieving distractions. Their energy is no longer drained by an attention that is constantly flitting here and there. Instead, their power of concentration has reached a point where they can choose where they wish to direct their attention. As a consequence, their breadth of awareness has increased beyond limitation.

accumulating gravity

Many cultures in the East place a strong emphasis on the role of the guru. *Guru* is a Sanskrit word that can be taken to mean "heavy." In the case of a teacher, it means "heavy with qualities." I think about these qualities as a kind of gravity. These are the positive qualities that such people have developed through their own efforts. The positive qualities have come to outweigh the negative ones. They have accumulated the kind of gravity that prevents them from being swayed by those old culprits.

We have the same potential. That is the point of practice: to make it possible to tilt the balance. We can overcome the pull of negativity and draw closer to the center of gravity that those seated figures represent. To accomplish this, we need to see the source of our distractions, both internal and external. We need to experience again and again how we are taken by these distractions. Each time we see we are taken, we have a moment when we can choose once more to turn back to ourselves.

The turning away from ourselves happens without our knowing. We are drawn by desires and we are repelled by fears. When we begin to regard ourselves, we often react negatively when we find we have been taken yet again. Such reactions themselves are another form of distraction.

I need to become more supple in seeing myself. I need more patience and generosity toward myself. I need to know that each time I find I am taken and choose in that brief moment to make the effort to return to myself, I have made a payment of attention.

Little by little, those payments will add up. It is like placing a drop of water into a bucket each day. It seems like nothing at first, but if we patiently continue, the bucket will fill. We should be careful not to set impossible goals for ourselves, where we are sure to fail and become discouraged. Rather, we can make small but steady efforts that will produce definite results in time.

The bees bring nectar from the flowers, one drop at a time. They place the drop into a cell of the honeycomb. They stand over the comb and fan the nectar with their wings to evaporate the water from it until more than ninety percent of it is gone, leaving only the essence. They repeat this again and again with each single cell of honey. Drop after drop. Flight after flight. Hundreds of thousands of drops. Millions of flights until slowly but surely they have filled the hive with golden honey.

the 84,000 delusions

We should rue no effort in the positive direction, no matter how small. The forces of negativity that we are subject to are so pervasive. The Buddha termed them the 84,000 delusions. We cannot expect to conquer them overnight. But we can eventually conquer them. Each payment of attention will go toward consciousness. Those payments are how we slowly but surely turn back the tide of negativity. That is what the silence of those seated figures tells us.

seeking out stillness

T ry to begin and end each day with a moment of stillness:

If you can take a moment to settle yourself before the rush of the day begins, it can act like an anchor, a reminder that there is silence even amid the flurry.

Before extinguishing the lights at the end of the day, look again for the stillness that was always there, even as you had to dash through the events of the day.

During the day, there are often opportunities to touch this silence, if only for a moment. Look for them, if you can, and take the moment for yourself. It requires no ostentation or special pose, just an acknowledgment that the silence is there. It is always there.

the compassionate gaze

chapter 11

In order to see the truth we need

*to view ourselves with **compassion**.*

The seated Buddhas I see in the museum speak of silence. They are no longer swayed by the force of negative emotions. But there is more. I am drawn to one sculpture in particular. It is in the Asian section of the Metropolitan Museum. It is a larger-than-life ceramic figure of a seated Lohan from fourteenth-century China. This figure bears a stern, compelling gaze that seems to be trained directly on the viewer. Standing before the figure, I feel illuminated. I don't mean that I feel particularly brilliant. I mean this figure represents the kind of gaze that illuminates every shadow: Nothing is hidden.

We know the phrase, "He sees right through me." This may seem daunting if I have something to hide. But when this gaze is combined with compassion, we begin to get some hint of what unconditional love might be like.

It is the kind of gaze that sees all the good qualities and all the faults and accepts them without judgment. It's the kind of gaze we need to cultivate toward ourselves. We need it so that we can see through the pretense of the ego and its absolute dependence on the negative emotions of greed, anger, pride, and jealousy. We need to see ourselves with compassion, as we are, without reacting in judgment. We need to see right through ourselves with the same kind of gaze that you can find on those figures in the museum. It's what I would call a gaze of dispassionate compassion.

In order to see the truth about ourselves, we need to look without conditions. Most of the time, we set conditions in our acceptance of others, subtle though they might be. We also set conditions for ourselves. Then we judge ourselves according to those conditions.

If only I can finish this chapter before I go to bed, I'll feel like I've done a decent day's work. But if I don't, I'll have frittered away another evening. What does that say about me and my abilities? Why can't I be more productive? Where else am I found wanting?

With this kind of thinking, I'm making my sense of self-worth conditional on finishing my work. When I don't meet the conditions, I tend to pass judgment on myself. Does that really make any sense? What purpose do these kinds of conditions really serve?

obstructed views

I think these conditions serve to further the machinations of the ego. I need to earn my keep in this world, it's true. If I set a begging bowl down in front of me, it would be a long wait before people came and filled it. But what does earning a living have to do with *me*, really? It's something I need to do, but it is hardly *me*. Yet these conditions are how I continue to define and prop up this identity. Good at this, bad at that. Coming up a little short here. Just managed to squeak by there. But each of these judgments misses the mark. They do not serve to expand my view. Quite the opposite. With each new criticism, I am mortaring another brick in the wall that blocks what I truly need to see—the unobstructed view of my real nature.

The Buddha gained such a view of the ego and expressed it quite clearly:

I have found you out, O Housebuilder.
I have torn down your walls and rafters.
I have come out of your house.
I am free at last.

Perhaps I can find a chink in the walls that hem me in, to see beyond my narrow self-interest to a more expansive view.

acknowledging dependence

Let's say your goal is to expand your view: To open your heart, to come more in contact with the whole of yourself. You might feel that right now you have a constricted view of yourself. Perhaps your view is constricted because you are unable to let go of this tight hold most of us have on our identity. Everywhere we turn, it seems to be reinforced by nagging reminders, not that "I am," but that I am "this" or "that." We use what we do to define who we are.

We do not really acknowledge our true dependence on the kindness of others. Because of this our own hearts are closed. We don't act with kindness and consideration because we are not aware of the kindness and consideration that has been showered on us our whole lives. We need to examine our situation:

I think about when I was an infant. I was totally helpless. I couldn't feed myself a single morsel. I couldn't walk or speak for myself. I was completely dependent. How could I have survived without the kindness and care of all those who took responsibility for me when I could not take responsibility for myself? People fed me and clothed me and taught me when I could do none of these things for myself. At that time, there was no way I could possibly pay them to do these things, yet they were all done for me. I hold that in my mind and look at the truth of that.

Sooner or later a feeling arises.

- *I am grateful for all the care I have been given.*

- *I have seen the truth of my situation.*

- *I have made a connection to something beyond my narrow view of myself and my needs.*

- *I am more in touch with my heart.*

Hold that feeling and try to experience it. You may begin to feel a wish to repay others for their kindness. You might see even the tired old phrase "It is better to give than to receive" in a different light. You might have a wish to act with more awareness, with more care and consideration. You have found a tiny chink in the wall that normally surrounds you. For a moment, you have come in touch with a more expansive view, seeing beyond the confines of the housebuilder.

the need
for practice

chapter 12

As with any true accomplishment,

*developing mindfulness requires **effort***

*and regular **practice**.*

ou could say that spiritual practice is a science. I mean this in the sense that science is the search for the truth. So is spiritual practice. Whereas science has trained its sights on the external world in its search, spiritual practitioners for thousands of years have turned their attention inward. But inner practice is conducted through experiment and observation, just as modern science is. In the end, they both have to arrive at the same point—the truth.

In science, a researcher poses a theory about the nature of the universe. Then, researchers conduct experiments in order to prove or disprove the theory. If the experiments can be reproduced by other scientists following the same methods and achieving the same results, the theory becomes accepted as truth.

Like science, spiritual practice is conducted by means of a series of experiments. Great beings before us have posed theories about the nature of existence. They have conducted experiments that led them on the path to enlightenment. Their explanations have been collected and made available over the centuries, just as scientists now publish their discoveries. In the case of Buddhism, these scientific works are known as the *dharma*. They provide a theory and a practice that lead to enlightenment.

The Buddha himself did not hesitate to experiment in pursuit of the truth. Nor did he hesitate to change his course when his experiments showed that he was headed down the wrong path.

the search for the truth

After he left his palace, Prince Siddhartha, the future Shakyamuni Buddha, traveled across India (with five fellow seekers) searching for teachings on the truth. Their search led them to undertake a path of extreme asceticism. For six years Shakyamuni fasted and practiced controlling his breath until his body grew emaciated and his strength had wasted away. His companions became alarmed at his decline. Still, Shakyamuni continued until his faculties and vitality nearly vanished. At this point, he had a vision of the god Indra playing a three-stringed harp. The first string was too loose and could produce no sound. The third string was too tight and snapped when plucked. It was only the correctly tuned middle string that could produce the desired sound. At that point he knew he must abandon his ascetic experiment and find a more balanced approach if he hoped to obtain enlightenment.

Our job, if we wish to pursue this path, is to slowly and patiently prove to ourselves the truth of these spiritual theories. We conduct the same experiments and follow the same path of others who have gone before us have, to see if we can achieve the same results.

The enlightened ones who have gone before us were no different from us. Otherwise, this kind of spiritual experiment would be useless. You'd have a hard job determining the properties of iron if your experiments were conducted on a piece of tin. But the Buddha was a human being just like us, with the same possibilities. He left a record of his method, just as other great teachers of the past have done. If the method is true and we follow it with similar effort, we should achieve the same results. But we have to apply ourselves to the task. Just reading about it will not produce the results.

applying yourself to practice

Science is based on the discovery of laws. The laws are the laws of nature that govern the material world. Spiritual practice is no different. It, too, is governed by laws. One basic law is that nothing comes from nothing. Another is that no one else can do it for you. In other words, as the lottery advertises, "You gotta be in it to win it." Simply reading about mindfulness is like reading about the lottery: You stand the same chance of collecting. That means you ' ave to apply yourself.

Self-realization means just that. You have to do it yourself through your own efforts. You can't buy it, and no one can hand it to you. If the enlightened beings—whose vow is to save all sentient beings—could save you by handing you enlightenment, they would have done it long ago. But they can't. The best they can do is to show you the way. You have to walk the path by yourself.

the importance of regular efforts

There is a reason why it's called practice. If you were trying to learn a skill—from playing the violin to fielding a fly ball— you would have to practice. That means repeating and perfecting your skills each day. Finding out what works and what doesn't, developing what works and discarding what doesn't. You would look into how others have succeeded. You would find a coach or a teacher to guide you and help you develop your skill. Your teacher would certainly admonish you to practice, not out of any egoistic aim but because he or she clearly understands that this is how you make progress.

I once heard a radio interview with the jazz saxophonist Sonny Rollins. He said he practiced for several hours every day. The interviewer asked him why he, such an accomplished performer, still felt the need to practice. Rollins explained that he once gave up practicing for several months. He had reached a point where he thought maybe it wasn't helping any more. Still in doubt, he stopped performing altogether.

Finally he had enough of this experiment. He picked up his instrument and began to play. The first problem was that his lip started bleeding. It had grown tender during the time off and could no longer withstand the rigorous demands of a musician of his caliber. He had to work his way back patiently. Then he offered up the real explanation for daily practice. It was so he could experiment, testing what he had learned and making it a part of himself. Then when he was on stage, the notes could be expressed without self-conscious effort. As he put it, he practiced so that when he performed he could "get out of my own way" and let the music play itself.

There is something to be said for making regular efforts. Some practice is better than none, since nothing comes from nothing. Regular daily practice is better than once a week or whenever the spirit moves you. But you should be cautious about forcing things and overdoing it. It is generally more productive to stop before you reach the point of tedium. Otherwise, you will be reluctant to take up the practice again.

I found training horses to be no different. If you could end the session just at the point where they were beginning to lose interest, they were more willing to begin training next time. Likewise, if you trained the horse one day but then slacked off for a week or two, there would be little progress. Our minds are not that different from those of unruly horses. We need regular, patient, insightful training—the kind of training that comes from regular practice.

making progress

Zen meditation retreats are called *sesshins*. They normally last for a week. The day begins at 4:15 A.M. with the sound of ringing bells. After a brisk walk, the participants take to their meditation cushions for the seated meditation practice of *zazen*. Every 45 minutes or so, the sittings are interrupted for ten minutes of walking meditation, called *kinhin*. This goes on with brief breaks for meals and a work session of cleaning and maintenance until 9:30 in the evening. There is no talking and no eye contact. After a certain amount of this, your knees begin to take notice.

Once each day, the Zen master, or *roshi*, gives what's known as a dharma talk. One talk I remember in particular spoke to the heart of how we make progress. At a certain point in the week, the state of the participants' knees must have been written on our faces. Looking out at us, the roshi related the words of his own late teacher, who had spent a lifetime in the practice of zazen. "In the first ten years, it is a struggle," he said. "In the next ten years, it becomes a habit," he continued. "In the next ten years, it becomes indispensable."

training your mind

You are training your mind. In order to do that, it behooves you to get acquainted with the subject you intend to train. That means getting to know your mind. In the beginning, the best way to accomplish that is simply to watch your mind. Your best opportunity to do that is to pause in your usual round of daily distractions and become quiet for a few moments. Stilling the body is part of that process, since it helps to still the external distractions of the mind. It is easiest to do that while seated. When you are lying down, sleep may be a little too available. Sitting is a position where you can remain at rest but alert. Even when you sit motionless, completely quiet, you are still breathing. That can be of help in maintaining awareness and focus.

Thoughts will come and go. In the sitting practice known as *shamata* ("concentrated meditation"), one suggestion is to recognize the thoughts as thoughts and let them go. Don't judge, recriminate, explain, or psychoanalyze. Just watch the untrained horse as it trots and tests the corral. Try to do this at a regular time each day for a few minutes at first, then maybe a little more after a while.

Know that right now this may be a struggle. But some day, not too far off, it will become a regular habit. Then, one day, you will find it is indispensable. As you watch the unruly colt romping about, know too that one day, with regular training and practice, you will ride that horse as swiftly as the wind, exactly where you choose to go.

going the distance

chapter 13

In choosing to develop mindfulness,

we have set ourselves a task that will not

be accomplished overnight. In order to

maintain the effort required without

getting "burned out," we need to practice

patience and enthusiasm.

If you look at anyone of accomplishment—whether it's a concert violinist, a champion figure skater, a renowned surgeon, or a spiritual teacher—you will probably find years of practice behind their accomplishment. What sustained them through the long hours? How did they keep from getting burned out?

First, they likely had a goal firmly in their minds. They knew where they wanted to go and they took pains to discover the best means of getting there. They had the patience to endure the obstacles and hardships in their way without succumbing to frustration and anger. They also had the enthusiasm that prevented them from getting burned out along the way. Their enthusiasm allowed them to continue making efforts because of the value and importance they placed on their goal.

Patience and enthusiasm are two of the six qualities or *paramitas* that traditional Buddhist teachings say should be perfected in order to make progress on the path. The other four qualities are generosity, moral discipline, concentration, and wisdom.

There is a distinction between conventional patience and the kind of patience meant by the paramitas. Regular patience will find you waiting all night by the telephone because your ex-girlfriend might call one more time. The patience we're referring to here is of a different order. It is the kind that overcomes the anger and frustration that arise when we are blocked from our goal.

In *A Guide to the Bodhisattva's Way of Life*, the eighth-century Indian saint Shantideva describes this kind of patience as something a little stronger than waiting for a telephone call. It is the patience that is the antidote to anger.

> *A single flash of anger destroys the good works*
> *of generosity and homage to the enlightened*
> *ones gathered in a thousand ages.*
> *There is no evil like hatred and no virtue like patience.*
> *Therefore earnestly cultivate patience in all ways.*[1]

pursuing patience

How do we attain this kind of patience? We do it by carefully examining the real situation. Buddhist teachings will bring up the example of a fellow with a stick. Suppose we are going merrily along, pursuing our noble aims. Then some mad person steps into the road and blocks our way. He is carrying a big stick and threatens to strike us. Perhaps he even succeeds, and we are whacked with the stick.

We get angry and want to topple this mad fool who dared to shout at us and even assault us. But what good does it do to get angry at the madman? He is completely controlled by his madness. If we look carefully, we will see that it is our own anger and frustration that have destroyed our happiness just then. If anything, we should be angry at the delusion that has dominated this poor fellow and robbed him of his own peace of mind.

Certainly we should protect ourselves and not suffer needlessly. We should also try to prevent this fellow from harming himself and others. But if we let our own anger control us and steal our happiness we are not much better off than the poor madman. Therefore we should develop patience to see through the slights and obstacles that beset us. We should not let them deter us from our goal. We turn this over in our minds until we are convinced of the need for patience—the anger-conquering patience rather than lovesick variety. That is how patience can support our mindful practice.

encouraging enthusiasm

Enthusiasm is also necessary. Without it we quickly grow tired and burned out. It is a long path we have undertaken. As the Buddha described it, we have set out to overcome 84,000 delusions. This kind of enthusiasm is also much more than the garden variety. As the *Offering to the Spiritual Guide* puts it:

> *Inspire me to perfect transcendent joyous effort*
> *By striving with tireless compassion for supreme enlightenment,*
> *Even if I must remain for many aeons*
> *In the deepest hellfires for the sake of each being.*[2]

Not too many of us would willingly take on that job. Even if we somehow landed up there, perhaps we could stand it for a fraction of a second. But joyfully? Yet that kind of enthusiasm is precisely what is required not only for the sake of others but for our own real happiness. We are not as far as we might think from that. It only requires setting our sights on the proper motivation. Think for a moment of the ceaseless rescue efforts in recent tragedies. In order to save even a single life, men and women worked relentlessly, day and night. They never gave up until every effort, no matter how difficult, was made. Undaunted, they worked until every life that could be saved was saved. No one had to order these people to their task. In fact, no one could turn them aside. They knew what was at stake and that knowledge gave them the kind of enthusiasm that no force on earth could vanquish. We have this strength within ourselves. Once we understand what is at stake we, too, will apply it.

Notes

1. Shantideva. *A Guide to the Bodhisattva's Way of Life.* Chapter VI: Verses 1–2. Author's own translation.

2. The First Panchen Lama Lozang Chokyi Gyaltsen (1570–1662). *The Offering to the Spiritual Guide (Lama Chopa).* Verse 69, tr. Gehlek Rimpoche.

boxing the shadow
of self-importance

I'm keeping an eye out for resistance. What is it that turns me away from attention? What is it that saps my enthusiasm and undermines my patience?

Work can be done willingly or grudgingly. This morning it was time to bundle the newspapers and take out the trash—a simple enough business, plainly necessary. Yet something tugs at me as I tie up the papers. Some irksome feeling spoils a bright blue-skied morning in the country. It's the nagging weight of resistance to the task at hand. An old habit rears its head and calls for attention.

If I trail this habit for a bit, I see it bears a resemblance to self-importance. Why must I do this? Don't I have better things to do? Why should I be fussing with this lowly twine?

Ah, there he is again: The thief who gulls me into complaint with the lure of self-importance. A peaceful morning, a reasonable task, an opportunity to pay attention to the work before me, but this cagey crook wants none of it. This is the one I'm after. This is what I need to see again and again—how my patience and enthusiasm are sapped by this shadow of self-importance.

This habit plays out in a constant calculation of who I think I am supposed to be and how that compares with where I think I should be on the ladder of accomplishment. It's an invidious comparison because it can never be fully met. It cannot be met because it is flawed in its basic premise. This is what I need to watch for if I wish to develop the kind of patience and enthusiasm that will sustain me on the path.

You can apply this patience to yourself or to someone else. When someone irks you, first become aware of the resistance rising from within:

- As strange as it sounds, is there something pleasurable in the irritation?

- Does the impulse to bare your teeth bring with it a taste for the fight? What was is it that is being irked?

- Where is your sense of self in this approaching fray?

- Do you feel something solid in the sense of the "I" who is rising to the outrage?

- What does this offended "I" stand to gain from this conflict?

Let's say you're sitting in the theater when someone behind you decides to unwrap a candy bar. The sound of the crackling cellophane threatens to drown out the hero's tender words up on the screen. What can patience do just then as the list of insulting remarks begins running through your head? After all, you shelled out your hard-earned cash to watch the show. Don't you have every right to watch the film in peace? Doesn't this numbskull realize the racket he's making? No one of your intelligence would ever be so oblivious. Why can't you just rid the world of all candy-crunching fools?

But try looking a little more closely at this dilemma. Did this fellow deliberately set out to get your goat? Probably not. Then who got the goat? Not the fellow with the candy, exactly. No, but the blame is already drawing uncomfortably close to the real goat-getter. In fact, I suspect he's sitting in my seat. Certainly, you have every right to ask for quiet in the theater. It's a commonly accepted convention. But next time, try leaving the goat at home.

the tools
at hand

chapter 14

Our busy lives seem to require

*so much of our **time** and **attention**.*

But seemingly harried activities present

*countless opportunities for **practice**,*

if we can learn to take advantage of them.

I was in the midst of writing this book, with barely six weeks left before the deadline, when Gehlek Rimpoche came to town. We had been working on another book, in a somewhat leisurely fashion, for over a year. It was difficult to find time to work with Rimpoche, so I made myself available.

I was glad to do it, but I was quite concerned about keeping to my schedule. I had a number of other pressing matters on hand, since I work freelance and deadlines are an ever-present part of the package.

Rimpoche comes from what he likes to call "good old Tibet." He says when he crossed the Himalayas into India during the Tibetan exodus of 1959, it was like being suddenly lifted from the sixteenth century into the twentieth. I take that to mean that deadlines were a novelty back there, because I have never seen him rush for anything.

That should have been my first clue when I went to meet Rimpoche for our first day of work. In my head, I could hear my own personal watch ticking away. I was anxious to know the plan, so I could schedule all my other work around it. This must have been as plain as a Times Square billboard to Rimpoche, because the first thing he said was, "I don't have a plan. You don't have a plan. Sometimes it's good to not have a plan."

For the next three weeks, we meandered around town, working on a few verses here and there, going out to lunch, going out to dinner. Watching a thunderstorm. More lunches. More dinners. We even included a trip to Chinatown where we stood on the street looking at the exotic fruits and vegetables.

The closest thing I could get to a timetable from him was some mention of twenty years for the book, with a hundred until the reviews came in. All the while, Rimpoche was making remarks about deadlines. He called them a form of laziness. He said that most of our contemporary busyness is a form of laziness. We use it as an excuse to keep the truly pressing priorities at the back of the line. We say we're too busy to find time to practice. But, in actuality, we always manage to find time for the things we want to do. It's what we give priority to that is the question.

working hard versus working smart

Without a doubt, we have to manage our lives. We live in a world where the vast majority of us have to pay our own way. Many of us have family obligations and other commitments. There's nothing wrong with that.

But there is a distinction between working hard and working smart. In the West, we seem to be famished for time. The clocks tick at the same rate as everywhere else; however, we are hard-pressed to meet a ceaseless torrent of demands on our time.

The more I think about it, the less working smart has to do with finding more time. It has to do with how I am using the time I have to balance the outer demands with the inner. It has more to do with quality than quantity. Because I live in the world and not as a meditator in some lonesome cave, why not approach every task for the opportunities it offers for inner work?

creating a sacred environment

Buddhism stresses the need for purification. We are all human and we all make mistakes. In spite of our best intentions, we wind up causing harm to ourselves and others. According to Buddhist philosophy, this creates negative *karma*. When the causes and conditions are right, the karma will ripen into unpleasant consequences. The act of purification can mitigate those consequences. Therefore, many practitioners are happy to have the opportunity to purify.

Cleaning is one very beneficial practice. In fact, it is the first instruction in the Tibetan *Lam Rim*, the teaching on the steps of the path to enlightenment. It is called creating a sacred environment. It literally means sweeping and cleaning the place where you intend to practice.

If, in this busy world, I find it difficult to spend adequate time on a cushion, then why not treat the places where I work as a sacred environment? Why not make the bed and wash the dishes and straighten my desk with that in mind? Why not approach all the tasks of the day mindfully? Why not make use of everything that comes to me in this same way? That would be working smart.

applying mindfulness to the mundane

Recognizing that you live in a time-famished age, it's to your advantage to make the best use of the opportunities at hand. Because you are obliged to pursue a number of seemingly mundane external activities each day, why not turn them to your inner benefit?

Take something as prosaic as washing the dishes. The meal is over and it's time to clean up. You remember your intention to practice mindfulness.

- *Your aim is to see beyond obscuration to the truth.*

- *You stand with your feet on the floor and a dish in your hand.*

- *You feel the weight of the dish.*

- *You attend to the sound of the water.*

- *You feel your feet on the floor. You are here.*

- *You breathe as you work. Your breath reminds you of your intention.*

You can work diligently or haphazardly. It is up to you. Why not apply yourself to the task? Quality in any work is a manifestation of attention. Because you wish to develop your attention, why not work in a way that fosters attention? It may appear to be a humble task, but the work of attention is not.

If you are slipshod in your effort here, how can you expect to be less than slipshod elsewhere? If pay attention to your work and do it well, you have a chance to glean the essence from it. You are preparing yourself through practice, making yourself ready. As you wash the dishes with attention, you are polishing your practice. No work done in this manner is wasted. Far from it. The practice builds by building on itself.

Perhaps, the next time you sit down to a meal with a clean plate before you, you will be reminded to be a little more mindful—to use this new activity, too, as practice.

part three

MIND

practicing mindfulness

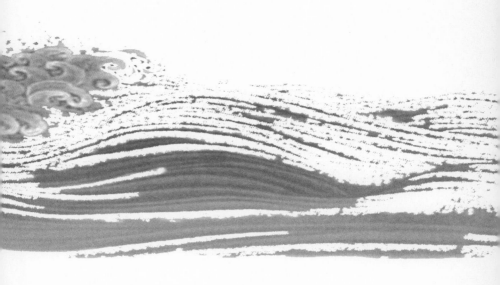

always present

*The **sensations** of the body are always present. Coming into **contact** with them brings us more clearly to the **moment**.*

We inhabit a sea of sensation. Our senses are awash in vibrations of sight, sound, smell, taste, and touch. This contact with the world produces a constant stream of reactions within us. We perceive this contact as pleasant, unpleasant, or neutral. We respond to those distinctions with like, dislike, or indifference. We are attracted to the sensations we like and averse to sensations we dislike. All this takes place in rapid succession, unbidden and often unperceived in most of us.

These sensations are always in the present moment. Yet we rarely seem to be. In the first instant of contact, our sensations give rise to feelings. But the chain of automatic reactions of like and dislike takes us farther and farther from these original, unbiased feelings.

There are many biological reasons for these reactions. They help the organism to survive by steering it from the painful to the pleasant. In most cases, what we perceive as pleasing has some biological merit, at least initially. We gravitate toward the sweet and away from the bitter. The calories contained in natural sugars sustain us. The alkali in bitter herbs warns us of potential toxins. Yet in our grosser nature, we quickly succumb to craving for the sweetness of one and aversion to the medicinal benefits of the other.

In his teachings on the Four Noble Truths, the Buddha spoke of craving as the cause of suffering. If we look carefully at this progression of reactions of the mind and body, we can begin to glimpse the mechanisms that give rise to craving.

They begin with sensation. These sensations are pervasive, but we rarely have direct, unclouded access to them. The sensations produce feelings of happiness, suffering or equanimity. These feelings lie at the source of our most basic motivation: to find peace and happiness and to escape suffering. If we can experience these feelings directly, without the shroud of ignorance, no craving will result.

Instead, we react to them. Shakespeare alludes to this when Hamlet, waxing philosophic, says, "Nothing is either good or bad, but thinking makes it so." We don't want to be separated from happiness. We want to avoid suffering. We want equanimity to remain. This seems normal on the face of it. After all, the wish for self-liberation is based on recognizing the nature of suffering and happiness. But craving takes us in the wrong direction.

countering cravings

Craving leads to grasping at what we think will free us from suffering and make us happy. But we suffer from ignorance about what will enable us to realize our goals. By not knowing the basic interdependent nature of reality and by not recognizing the consequences of our actions, we set off on a course that produces the unhappy results brought by attachment and aversion. If you're looking for the marauding thief who steals our happiness, this place of craving is where he saddles his horse.

It is said there is no difference between the mind of the Buddha and the body of the Buddha. Enlightenment means total awareness, free from the reactions of ignorance. Certainly most of us are far from that level. But we can begin to cultivate this awareness through sensation. It is available to us at every instant—there, in the present, in the body.

If we begin to attend to these sensations, we can come closer to seeing the mechanism of our reactions. Seeing without habitual reaction is awareness. With awareness, we are on the trail of the thief.

focusing on sensation

You can develop awareness by focusing your attention on sensation. Most teachings will tell you to begin with the breath:

- *As you sit quietly, try to focus your attention on the breath as it leaves your body.*

- *With your mouth closed, sense the breath passing through the nostrils.*

- *Follow each breath. Some teachers suggest counting the breaths from one to ten. Monitor your progress and be honest with yourself. If you find you have drifted off, go back to one and start counting again. Be honest but watch for the reaction of self-criticism.*

- *There is a subtle moment, when you find yourself far from your breath, where a reaction may take place. Watch this reaction. Does it take you farther or closer to yourself? Look for hoof prints of the thief on his horse. Return to the breath.*

- *It is said that a Buddha's awareness pervades every cell of the body. Practice sensing this vast inner landscape. This is the landscape of the central nervous system. Buddhist physiology describes the nervous system as a network of channels, some 72,000 in all. While sitting quietly, turn your attention to your hand, your foot, your spine. Dive deeply and try to experience what you discover. Watch carefully. Take note of the sensations, the feelings, the reactions. Develop awareness.*

- *Continue this practice during the day. As you walk, decide to pay attention to your feet on the ground for the distance of a block. Listen to the sounds enveloping you. Again, watch the reactions of like and dislike, of attraction and aversion.*

- *Try dividing your attention in this way as you go through the activities of the day, saving one part of your attention for sensation as you move or speak or listen.*

If you practice in this way, returning again and again to the sensations of the moment, little by little you will come to taste what it means to be aware. It is the taste of joy.

raising
a joyful sound

*Our negative and positive activities take place through **body**, **speech**, and **mind**. Mindfulness of speech offers insight in how our speech affects others and how the speech of others affects us.*

The element of speech presents many levels for mindful cultivation. We can use the vibration of sound to develop our awareness by observing where the voice comes from as we speak. By following our sensations, we can get a sense of our state of tension or relaxation. By listening to ourselves, we can become aware of the motivation behind our words.

We can look carefully to see how we affect others through our speech. Do we use speech to help or to harm? Kind words, jealous words, harsh words, soothing words all speak to whether we are pursuing a positive or negative direction. What lies behind those harsh words? Pride, anger, or jealousy? If we can learn to listen to ourselves, we can begin to hear the demanding cries of the ego behind our negative expressions. What does the tone of the voice convey? Where does the voice come from in those moments of anger or imprecation? See if it is possible to sense its place of tension. We can follow the sound of our own words back to their source to learn more about the truth of how we are.

We can also follow the reactions within ourselves in response to the speech of others. How swiftly we are pricked by sharp speech. How quickly we rise to the defense. How ready we are to strike back with wounding words of our own. How many times has the world been led into madness or danger through the negative power of speech? How much suffering has been engendered through words of hatred? We would do well to choose our words carefully considering the havoc they can wreak.

Kind words bring another spectrum of response. We light up to praise. We are comforted by kindness. Speech can be a powerful force for the positive.

Speech is the principal messenger we use to convey the truth. We depend on the words of the great teachers to find our way along the path. While these teachers are no longer present in the body to offer guidance, their enlightened speech remains, transmitted over space and time through written text and oral tradition.

experiencing the sound of truth

Truth has a way of touching us when we are open to it. We can be touched to the heart by words that ring true. In such moments, we are more in contact with the whole of ourselves. We hear and feel things in a different light.

Most of our listening occurs through a filter of criticism. We are pushed and pulled by speech—snagged by the words of others and mesmerized by our own—so that at times we seem to be talking in our sleep.

Try to listen for this honestly. Do you really know what you're talking about or do you sound more like you're talking through your hat?

When we learn to become more open, we have the possibility of listening in stillness. At its ultimate level, speech approaches silence. We can learn to listen to the stillness behind the words. All this is part of the practice of mindful speech.

Chanting and singing have been used in many cultures in the practice of mindfulness. Chanting offers ample opportunity to gauge how our thoughts drift and return during the chant. The Sanskrit word *mantra* means "mind protection." Consider how mindful speech can serve as protection for the mind. Mindful speech keeps us in the present moment. If we are mindful with our words, we cut off one avenue for the expression of negativity. It keeps us honest.

avoiding mindless, thoughtless speech

None of us wishes to be the recipient of mindless, thoughtless words. Buddhist teaching describes four types of negative speech: lies, divisive speech, harsh words, and idle gossip. This kind of speech is like poison. It can affect the listener and the speaker both. Consider how abusive speech alone, with never a raised hand, can afflict children and destroy marriages. Gossip can become an addiction that can undermine a reputation, ruin someone's livelihood, and sully a good name. Lying can lead to tragic consequences. People poisoned with falsehood can turn to hatred. People falsely accused suffer injustice. People misled by untruthful words can waste their lives in false pursuits. Divisive speech creates conflicts great and small.

Consider whether your words fall into any of these categories. If we want to avoid tainting our minds with the poisons of negative speech, we would do well to speak mindfully.

finding a truthful tone

Try to truly *listen* as you speak.

Begin with the sensation of the sound. See where your voice is centered:

• Is it in your throat or head or from somewhere lower down?

Try to perceive the tension or relaxation your speech produces
within yourself.

Follow your words:

• How are they inflected?

• Are they forced or easy?

Listen for the stresses:

• Is the tone high or low pitched?

• What does that tell you?

Analyze what you are doing:

• Are you trying to make a point or to make yourself heard?

• Or are you also trying to manipulate a response in the other person?

Most of us have a subtext when we speak, which is the message we really wish to convey. Can you hear it in yourself? Can you hear it in others? We may wish to speak straightforwardly, but fear and desire prevent us from openly speaking our minds. What does such speech sound like? How does it feel? Is it your true voice or is it constrained in some way?

If you listen to someone singing, you immediately hear the difference between a voice that is free and one that is forced or self-conscious. You can hear when the song is heartfelt and when is it false.

- *If you have the heart for it, try raising your own voice in song.*

- *Try to sense the source of self-consciousness and the constraints singing imposes.*

- *Try to feel the difference, should you happen to "find your voice."*

- *If you have the opportunity, try singing with others.*

- *Listen for the moment when your voice joins with the others—when it flows freely, when there is no longer a difference between the singer and the song.*

taming the
wild horse

chapter 17

Our minds are capable of extraordinary

accomplishment, *if we learn how*

to tame them to the useful work

*of **self-awareness**.*

Atisha, the great Buddhist teacher from twelfth-century India, said, "When in company, check your speech. When alone, check your mind."

As we are, our minds are hampered by delusion. Ignorance is the root of our delusions. The Buddha taught that true freedom requires wisdom. Wisdom is the only way to cut ignorance once and for all. Wisdom can be acquired only through the power of concentration. The stabilized mind of concentration depends on freeing ourselves from the pull of negative addictions.

Mindfulness is the awareness of actions, words, and thoughts. All three realms hold the potential for positive and negative activity. Lacking awareness, we are prone to thoughtless action. We have all experienced the damage wrought by careless words and actions at one time or another. Because they are the source of negative words and actions, mindless thoughts can be equally damaging.

Habitual tensions in the body are a consequence of a lack of awareness. The habitual thinking that many of us are subject to is also the result of a lack of awareness. When we turn our attention to our thoughts, we begin to see how capricious and unruly they appear. Instead of being guided by intention, most of the time our thoughts are pushed and pulled by delusion. Traditional teachings describe six principal delusions: ignorance, attachment, anger, pride, wrong views, and doubt.

These delusions create trouble for us. Each one of them has the stickiness of habit as part of its nature. Like habits, they seem effortless to acquire and difficult to shake. Habitual tensions in the body do us no good. They waste our energy and lead to all manner of physical side effects. Deluded thoughts produce similar results in our mindstream, draining our strength of attention and racking the inherently calm nature of the mind with turbulence. We lack the power of concentration because our minds are constantly pushed and pulled by these addictive thoughts. We need concentration to develop the wisdom necessary to eliminate the thief and his depredations once and for all. But these habitual delusions block us.

wrestling with wrong views

Doubt hinders our progress by compelling us to tread the same ground over and over. Rather than questioning a point, examining it, deciding upon its validity, and then applying it to our practice, we circle around and around so that we can no longer rely on our intelligence and experience. If we do not trust our intelligence and our own experience, we can never hope to find our way out of the forest of delusion.

Anger consumes our peace of mind until we are completely overpowered by its fury. We cause great harm to ourselves and others. Like a raging fire, it destroys in moments what has taken years to build.

Wrong views block our progress by clouding our minds with ideas that will never produce the results we need. Wrong views represent the other extreme from doubt. Instead of endless questions, we accept dubious notions without properly examining them. In its worst case, this can lead to the kind of blind faith that produces tragically fatal consequences for its misguided followers.

Pride holds us back by trapping us in a false view of ourselves. Drunken with our own infallibility, we are unable to observe and question our actions. We become blind to our negative motivations, wandering farther and farther from the truth.

Attachment holds our minds prisoner with craving. We cannot let go of our grasping thoughts. When we are in their grip, greed, jealousy, and covetousness goad us night and day. The pull of these desires dominates our thoughts so that we can never achieve the calm balance necessary to develop concentration and wisdom.

Ignorance is at the root of all these delusions. Because we cannot see and understand the nature and source of delusions, we are doomed to remain in their grip. Ignorance blocks our view by presenting an entirely false one in its stead. We believe the view that ignorance presents and we cease to question what lies at the heart of our troubles. This is how the thief hides and protects himself, shrouded behind the mirage of ignorance.

dealing with delusion

As Atisha said, we need to check our minds. We need to develop the stability that makes wisdom possible. That means training this powerful but unruly horse so that it can carry us where we need to go.

Patient, steady practice is the best way to accomplish this. As long as the mind is disturbed by negative thoughts, it will be difficult to train. If you were training a horse, you would empty the corral of other wild, young horses that would cause interference and distraction. In the early stages of your practice, you can similarly rid your mind of distraction by concentrating on the breath. Most of us cannot easily hold more than one thought in our minds at the same time. By concentrating on the reality of the breath, you gradually rid your mind of disturbing influences.

When you have achieved a more quiet state, begin to contemplate the nature of your delusion. When you are attempting to conquer delusions, the traditional teachings suggest focusing on your principal delusion first. The reason is that if you were being attacked by a gang of thieves and you had to strike one first, you would go for the leader. If the leader falls, the rest will lose heart. Each of us is under the sway of some principal delusion. For some it is anger. For others, pride. Some may be obsessed with attachment.

*Get to know which of these thieves holds sway over your mind. Focus on its
nature. Examine whether it can possibly free you from suffering. Determine
whether it will bring about lasting happiness. Can you honestly say that you
are in control of this delusion or does the delusion control you?*
*When you find the answers to these questions, you can begin to build the
determination within yourself to break free of delusion's domination. You will
begin to realize:*

This delusion has robbed me of joy time and time again. I have lived under its
control for most of my life. It has brought me nothing but trouble. It has
stood in the way of my progress. It has brought suffering to myself and
others. But now that I have seen its true cost, I will no longer tolerate it.
From this moment on, I will be fiercely vigilant so that it never again steals
from me my precious peace of mind.

As Shantideva said:

> *Time and again examine*
> *The state of your body and mind*
> *To be brief: the nature of vigilance*
> *Is that of a sentry.*

the three poisons and their antidotes

*The negative emotions of **anger**, **attachment**, and **ignorance** rule our thoughts. Mindful practice can help us develop powerful antidotes to these three poisons.*

The great Buddhist teacher Shantideva urged us to examine the state of our body and mind. Our state is our guide, directing us to where we need to work. It's safe to say our work lies in freeing ourselves from the three basic negative addictions: anger, attachment, and ignorance.

The Buddha taught that we are each responsible for ourselves. Our state, whether joyful or miserable, is entirely our own making. But as long as we are unable to realize that, it is tempting to place the blame elsewhere. At times, this finger-pointing appears to be convincingly justified. Suppose I have an enemy who would like to see my undoing. That angry, howling fellow is certainly a cause of my discomfort. Without him in the picture, I would be happy and at peace. I clearly see him as the cause of my trouble. If some unfortunate accident befell him, wouldn't I be pleased? After all, it would serve the fool right. In fact, the world would be well rid of him and his abuse. I'd arrange it myself if I thought I could get away with it. I'd be doing everyone a favor.

But does this kind of thinking bear up to scrutiny? It's clear at a glance that this person with the distorted face who rants and bellows at me is completely controlled by his anger. His mind is poisoned by it. He is trying to spread his poison to me. Won't I be the fool if I willingly drink it in? When someone is poisoned, does it make sense to be angry with the person when the poison is to blame? The poison of anger has made him mad. Should I be angry with a madman? Or is his madness a more fitting target?

By mindfully watching my reactions, I can begin to anticipate them. The next time they arise, I can try to intercept the poison before it spreads to my own mind. If I am paying attention, I can apply the antidote to anger before I, too, am infected. The antidote is patience. Patience allows me to see anger for the thief it is. I can use my mind to cut through anger's red haze to see the truth. I can continue my practice, remaining quietly vigilant for the signs of the thief.

the perils of attachment

Attachment is the sticky stuff that drives us to distraction. We can't let go and we can't get enough. We pin our hopes of happiness to the object of our attachment. Instead, we derive our misery from it. Attachment robs us of the ability to appreciate what is worth appreciating. We are fearful of losing what we have and afraid of not getting what we want. It is difficult to appreciate something if you live in fear of losing it. This fear produces constant turbulence in our minds. It propels us to grasp at what is in fact ungraspable. We try to keep and hold objects, hoping they will bring us joy by their possession. But those objects are all impermanent. My splendid little house in the country is slowly but surely returning to the earth. The roof leaks in the winter. I can repair it, but then the boiler breaks down. I can also fix that, but the trees in the front yard are aging and dying. I can plant new trees, but will I be around long enough to see them mature? Wouldn't it be better to relax my grip and appreciate what lies before me?

How much more impossible is our attachment to others? If I pin my happiness on making someone mine, how well will that succeed? In my heart, I behave as if I own the other person, as if they exist to make me happy. But to do this, they have to conform to my idea of how they should behave.

If I judge them by my standards instead of accepting them for themselves, I will be constantly disappointed. We are changing all the time—our likes and dislikes, our hairlines and our waistlines. If they turn their affections away from me, I am either outraged or devastated. Attachment plays Iago to my Othello, goading me into madness. The news is rife with such consequences of attachment.

Attachment steals our contentment. The Buddha taught that our chief dissatisfaction comes from not being content with what we have. Attachment can run riot with our minds once we are infected with its poison. We need to mindfully pay attention to its symptoms and apply the antidote. The antidote is the deep recognition of the impermanent nature of what we desire. By seeing that we cannot truly possess what we desire, we can relax our frenzied pursuit. By relaxing our fearful grasping, we become free to appreciate what we have.

understanding ignorance

Ignorance is at the root of these negative addictions. Ignorance prevents us from seeing that nothing exists independently. Because of its interdependent nature, everything that exists is also impermanent.

This means that nothing, including the ego, exists in and of itself. It is all comprised of components. This person sitting here typing is the combination of a body, a consciousness, and a name. Take away any one of those and I no longer have this identity. This is a difficult fact for the ego to swallow. The ego likes to view itself as entirely independent, relying on nothing for its existence. If it depends on something for its existence, then it always stands the risk of annihilation. This produces the pervasive fear that underlies most of our actions.

The wisdom that sees the true nature of reality is what cuts ignorance at its root. It finally frees the mind of its last hindrance.

As the *Heart Sutra* says:

The Bodhisattva relies on highest perfect wisdom
With no hindrance in the mind.
No hindrance, therefore no fear.
Far beyond upside-down views.
At last nirvana.

Nirvana is freedom from suffering. It's the fear and confusion of ignorance that is the root of all our suffering. Eradicating this profound ignorance is a tall order. It's about the tallest order there is. The wisdom described in the *Heart Sutra* lies at the end of a long, long road of effort and practice. But the path is there. And the teachings are there to guide us. Our own minds are what will ultimately realize the truth. We all have that potential.

love versus attachment

We all wish for love, to feel love and to express it. Even the most hardened heart is closed only because it lacks love. But attachment often masquerades as love. It is only when it is put to the test that we see its true colors. We need to learn to discern delusion from the truth.

Ask yourself to honestly answer the following questions:

- *Does your love for others rely on some kind of implicit bargain?*

- *Do you love them because they love you?*

- *If you do something for them, do you expect something in return?*

- *If someone you profess to love were to grow old or infirm, would your feelings change?*

- *What if their happiness depended on their moving to the other end of the earth and never seeing you again? Would you welcome their move because it would make them happy? Or does your love exist only if your lover meets certain conditions?*

putting anger in the dock

Most of us justify our anger by placing blame on the object of our anger.

- *Try to follow this trail of blame. Look into it as if you were a private investigator on the case of some major swindle.*

- *Would your blame stand up in court or is your anger part of some cover-up?*

- *Build your case diligently and thoroughly. Take evidence.*

- *Put your anger on the stand and force it to testify.*

- *Who's behind it?*

- *What is the motive?*

- *Who benefits?*

- *How do they benefit?*

- *Who is the victim?*

- *Who gains?*

- *Who suffers?*

banishing ignorance

Ignorance is the source of our delusions. They are addictions. Try to get a feel for these negative emotions when they arise.

- *Every addiction has a pleasurable component. If anger rises, try to sense the subtle pleasure in the center of the fury.*

- *When you're suffering because the object of your attachment lies just beyond your reach, see if you can taste the odd sweetness at the center of your misery.*

- *Look into all your obsessions in this way. See if that sense of pleasure in the midst of delusion is reinforcing something inside you. See if it reflects your sense of yourself.*

- *Is there a part of you that identifies itself as the heartbroken one or the furious one or the longing one?*

- *See if you are using the delusion in some subtle way to define yourself.*

- *Then ask yourself if that is really you.*

suspending
judgment

*We tend to view the world through the filters of **like**, **dislike**, or **indifference**. Mindful practice can help us see things clearly as they are, by freeing us from habitual reactions.*

Alot of the business of Zen is conducted through *koans*, collections of teaching stories that usually contain a paradoxical twist. The Sufi branch of Islam also contains a wealth of stories used to reveal the truth. One popular series of stories features Mullah Nasrudin, the odd-witted Sufi saint. His chief characteristic is that he embodies the qualities of the wise fool. In one old story, a friend comes along one night to find Mullah Nasrudin on his hands and knees on the street in front of his house. He is searching the ground underneath a lamppost. The friend asks the mullah what he is doing. The mullah replies that he has lost the key to his house. His friend asks the mullah where he had last seen the key. "In the house," the mullah answers. "Then why are you searching under the lamppost?" the friend asks. "More light," the mullah replies.

We're engaged in a similar business here, and seeing is the key. In order to see properly, we need more light. At the moment, our vision is obscured by preconceptions and habitual judgments. We have to learn to suspend those judgments. We normally see the world through a filter of preconception. How many times have you mislaid your own keys and—certain they were somewhere else—missed seeing them right under your nose? We tend to see what we want to see and diligently avoid seeing what we would prefer not to see. This not-seeing becomes ever more exaggerated when it comes to looking at ourselves.

When I look in the mirror, I am viewing a composition of preconceptions. I see myself as a collection of identities and labels, a series of seminal stories that define who I think I am. I rely on my relationships with others to reinforce this patchwork sense of self. The whole apparatus is designed to prevent me from seeing myself as I am.

But that's not the half of it. Everything I see in this cursory self-examination is tainted with judgment. I don't mean that we should not be discerning. Quite the opposite. We need to become sharply discerning in the search for the truth. When I say tainted, I mean it in the sense that our judgments are colored by fears, preconceptions, and habits. If I look carefully, I see I am almost compelled to pass judgment on everything with which I come into contact. At a very basic level, our perceptions are subject to a torrent of likes and dislikes. It is very difficult to simply perceive what is.

the need for more light

The thief we must destroy is sustained by these judgments. Take the case of greed. Greed can never be satisfied because it demands the whole world. When we are unable to deliver up the whole world, this tyrant flies into a rage. We feel sick and dissatisfied because we have been unable to meet the ego's demands. We feel inadequate, undone. We turn on ourselves until we become the object of our own abuse. One of the unfortunate side effects of this process is bitterness. If you watch, you can see this drama being played out all around you. If you look carefully, you may find that you may even be playing a hand in it yourself.

Discernment means seeing with an eye for the truth. The truth is not based on like or dislike, attraction or aversion. The truth is what is. The most important truths in the business at hand are not based so much on what we see as on how we see it. No more so than when we train this eye upon ourselves. We are looking for the key. This is the point the mullah makes: We need more light.

We need to look at ourselves and see the truth. But our looking needs to be mixed with compassion. Otherwise, we can fall into the trap of self-denigration.

Most of us are pretty touchy when it comes to criticism from the outside. It can sometimes be easy for others to "push our buttons," which causes us to emit a melodious howl. But our "buttons" only function because we believe some falsehood about ourselves.

When someone "gets" to us, they are pointing to a misconception that we believe about ourselves. Otherwise, they would have no power over us. Can you imagine pushing the Buddha's buttons? No, because enlightened beings see only the truth. The buttons are falsehoods we have come to believe and even defend. But the truth frees us of these false convictions. No would-be button pusher can hold sway over us then.

We need to see the truth in order to take advantage of the freedom it offers. That's why we need to suspend our habitual judgments in favor of a more discerning view.

handling harmful delusions

Part of the discerning view of ourselves means we need to see the nature of our actions clearly. Are they positive or negative? Are they causing harm to ourselves or others? If they are, we need to correct them. But not through chastisement. If you had a beloved child who was endangering itself, you would make efforts to correct it for its own good. That would be your responsibility. But you would do it out of love and compassion, not from some urge to punish. It's the same method we can apply to ourselves.

Buddhist teachings suggest applying the four "R's" when we suspect that we have caused harm to ourselves or others.

They are:

1. **Recognition:** We first need to recognize the nature of our action. If it is negative, we need to see that and understand why it is harmful. We should examine how it has caused harm or brought suffering to someone, including ourselves.

2. **Regret:** Once we recognize that we have caused harm, we must contemplate what we have done until we have developed a feeling of regret from the bottom of our hearts. This is beyond sentiment. It arises from seeing the truth of suffering and our role in it.

3. **Resolution:** When we see and regret the suffering we have caused, we will become determined not to let this happen again. We will grow strong in our wish to be free from the delusion that led us to cause harm.

4. **Reparation:** Once we have resolved to root out this harmful delusion, we can work to repair the damage by practicing generosity and patience. We can also work toward developing our compassion so that we will no longer act in a way that harms ourselves or others. This will put us firmly on the path of mindfulness.

chasing the
thief on his
own horse

chapter 20

Suffering robs us of our equanimity.

Through mindfulness, we can learn

to use suffering as a tool on the path

to *awareness*.

The Buddha was raised as a prince. A soothsayer had told his father that his young son would either become a great monarch or an enlightened being. The king preferred to have an heir to his throne. So he provided his son with every earthly pleasure possible, hoping to bind his son to royal life and distract him from the truth of the world that awaited him outside the palace walls. But Siddhartha grew weary of the glut of pleasure. He suspected there was more to life. He asked a groom to escort him from the palace in secret.

The king had been thorough in shielding the prince from the truth. The first time the prince ever came upon sick, elderly, and dying people was on his forays outside the palace. At first, he had no idea what he was witnessing and had to ask the groom to explain what he was seeing. But as he looked more deeply, he realized that no living being was free from these ultimate afflictions. He decided to devote his life to determining whether there was a way out of this unhappiness.

Unlike Prince Siddhartha, we don't have to go out of our way to discover suffering. We may be lulled to sleep by momentary comforts and pleasures, but the truth is right on the other side of the wall. It doesn't require seeing the sufferings of sickness, old age, and death. A wayward glance by a lover, the embarrassment of a bounced check, or the headache brought on by a harsh word from the boss are enough to show us the temporary nature of happiness.

Suffering can help us develop mindfulness and mindfulness can help us end suffering. It may seem strange, but ease can be an obstacle to mindfulness and thus to awakening. When we are happy and comfortable, we are apt to be complacent. When we are suffering and experiencing firsthand the nature of life and death, we begin to realize that we must do something to help ourselves. Like a prisoner who is held in an unbearable prison, we develop a fierce determination to free ourselves from the conditions that cause us to suffer. Once we have that kind of determination, no obstacle can withstand our resolve.

a useful approach to suffering

So what is a useful approach to suffering? As we work toward the determination to free ourselves from suffering, mindfulness is our most important tool.

First, we can use mindfulness to determine whether the suffering is avoidable. If the suffering can be alleviated by a heart-to-heart talk, a little bit of financial planning, or an aspirin, then, by all means, alleviate it. There is enough suffering to go around. There is no benefit to suffering needlessly. If there is no way around it, then mindfulness can help us recognize that fact.

Second, if a mindful examination of the situation leads us to conclude that the suffering is unavoidable, there is not much use in suffering over the fact that we're in for some suffering. One suffering is quite sufficient.

Some years ago, I was trying to put together a movie deal. I had written the screenplay but I had never directed a feature film before. I managed to get a movie star attached to the project and to make an appointment with the studio that was to produce it. The head of the studio was a notoriously belligerent person and I was certain he was going to challenge my fitness for the work. I figured I was in for it. I spent the morning before the big meeting wandering up and down the Santa Monica beach. How was I going to get through this in one piece?

Then it occurred to me. If I was going to suffer anyway, then why not suffer cheerfully? It seemed strange, at first, putting those two words together. But by the time I got to the meeting I was repeating "suffer cheerfully" like some kind of mantra. The meeting went better than I had imagined. We made the deal and they bought the project.

That night I took the red-eye flight back to New York, pleased with my new "mantra." We took off. They lowered the lights for the long flight home. The flight attendant came down the aisle asking if anyone was willing to give up their pillow. "Suffer cheerfully," I thought, as I handed her my pillow. By the time we landed in New York, I had an exquisitely stiff neck. That's when I learned the second half of the mantra. Suffer cheerfully, sure; but don't suffer needlessly.

If we do have to suffer, at least we can try to bring mindfulness to the suffering. Suffering is an immediate reminder of the present moment. We are fortunate in that respect: We can suffer only in the present moment. Physical suffering is obvious. But mental and emotional suffering share this quality of immediacy. We can spend hours ruing some unpleasant moment from the past or fretting over some slight we fear might happen in the future, but the actual suffering is taking place right now.

Suffering is also temporary. A simple examination of past suffering shows this. A deeper analysis will lead to an understanding of the impermanent nature of all such phenomena. If we are going to suffer, at least let's be accurate about its nature. Just as there is enough suffering to go around, we also don't need to give suffering qualities it doesn't deserve. Immortality is certainly not one of them.

At the very least, let suffering be a reminder that you are alive in the present moment and that the suffering is by its very nature impermanent. It will end. If we can grasp these understandings, we can start to turn the tables on suffering.

using mindfulness to counter suffering

Here, again, mindfulness is the key. Ask yourself: What part of me, exactly, is suffering? My toe? The tip of my toe? Is my toe all there is to me? Or am I suffering in my heart because my lover scorned me? Where is my "heart"? Where does the suffering end and I begin? Who is this person who is suffering, anyway? How did I get into this mess and how am I going to get out of it? Maybe I should begin to cultivate a little mindfulness and see what this suffering is really all about.

The late William Segal was one of the first Americans to visit the Zen monasteries in Japan after World War II. Once he told me about the time he was in a terrible car accident. He nearly died in the wreck and had to undergo many operations to reconstruct his broken body. As he was lying in his hospital bed, Soen Nakagawa Roshi, the renowned Zen master, came to visit him. "Lucky, lucky man," Soen Roshi said, taking Mr. Segal's hand. "One accident like yours is worth ten thousand sittings in a monastery."

As Mr. Segal put it, "In the hospital, I came to an attitude of appreciation for the smallest things. My jaws had been wired shut and when they were finally released so that I could manage to suck through a straw, the sensation of a fluid going down my throat filled me with gratitude."

Through his suffering he came to see beauty in the everyday lives of people. He would watch the man who cleaned at night and sometimes the two would exchange a few words. The man was a recent immigrant who had taken the only job he could get. How carefully and conscientiously he worked. How economical his movements were. There was in every gesture the nobility of doing what life required of him.

"One takes everything for granted until it's taken away," Mr. Segal added. "If one has a relatively good body and mind, one is proud of 'my' strength and 'my' intelligence. It doesn't take much to show the falsehood of that. One small blow and they're gone. Whatever could be taken away so easily couldn't have belonged to me. It all added up to a humbling, chastening experience. Best of all, it brought a new level of tolerance in my attitude toward others."

Normally, we turn away from pain. We protect ourselves by drifting away from the present moment. If the pain becomes too much, we faint. Mental trauma can have the same result. We block it out because it becomes too much to bear. There's nothing wrong with that. It's a natural protection of the nervous system. But it is also a habit, one we use in less traumatic circumstances to keep from facing the real question of what is causing our suffering. Knowing and understanding the nature of suffering can be a tremendous help in cultivating mindfulness along the path to freedom.

When Jesus was about to take leave of his disciples at the Last Supper, he knew they would have to face great suffering in the days ahead. He told them:

In the world ye shall have tribulation,
but be of good cheer; I have overcome the world.

a meditator's trick

When encountering suffering, my own teacher, Gehlek Rimpoche, uses what he calls a meditator's trick. Rimpoche suffers from diabetes. Because of this, he must inject himself with insulin every day. By his own admission, the needle hurts. Instead of simply putting up with the pain, he takes advantage of the situation. Since he is going to suffer from diabetes anyway, he says, he asks that he be able to take on all the diabetes for the entire world so that no one will ever have to suffer from diabetes again.

- *You can try this trick the next time you're suffering. If you suffer from migraine and you've tried all the remedies at hand and still you're experiencing pain, then let it be for some good. Since you have to suffer anyway, then let it be for all the migraine sufferers in the world, so that no one will ever have to bear this miserable affliction again.*

- *If your lover has left you behind and you are suffering the heartache we all know, then let it be for all the heartbroken ones in the world, so they will never have to bear the pain of loneliness again.*

- *Remember that this wish includes yourself, too. You are one of the heartbroken ones. You, too, are the diabetic or the migraine sufferer. In your mindfulness, you are wishing for us all to be free.*

Rimpoche calls it a meditator's trick. I call it chasing the thief on his own horse.

why is the buddha smiling?

chapter 21

*We are on the trail of the **thief** who steals our **joy**. What happens when we finally catch him?*

The Buddha set out 2,500 years ago to find the path to liberation. For the Buddha liberation meant freedom from suffering. He looked into the nature of reality, searching for the cause of suffering and the way to end it. He saw that everything that we rely on for happiness is impermanent. He saw that when we fail to understand this fact, we become consumed with craving for what we believe will make us happy. Beyond that, we grasp at our own identity, our sense of self. We believe it is something permanent and independent of this changing, impermanent world. At the deepest level, we accept this appearance of our "I" as the truth. The Buddha looked into the heart of this acceptance and saw it was false.

His discovery is that there is no independent self. Certainly we exist. Someone suffers from negative addictions. Someone works to free themselves. Someone is liberated. But how we think we exist is the source of the confusion. The true "I" is dependent on the combination of mind and what the Buddha called the five *skandas* or aggregates. These are traditionally taught as the component elements that comprise a human being: form, feeling, thought, volition, and consciousness. A contemporary way of looking at it is that we are the combination of mind and genetics, two streams flowing through time and intersecting—mind and DNA.

Grasping at an independent identity is the source of all our fear and confusion. It is the cause of all our suffering. This is what the Buddha saw. When he finally trained his wisdom on the source of this suffering, he saw it did not exist. It never existed. We only believe that it does, and that fundamental falsehood leads us astray.

the thief who never was

There is no thief. But because we accepted his existence, we have been dominated our entire lives. It is like a bullying father who cows the family into silence. It is like a tyrant who has terrorized the people into submission. It is like the Wizard of Oz making his outlandish demands. Seeing him for what he is eliminates him, because he was never there.

It may seem unsettling at first, this collective, impermanent self. But if you stay with it, it is liberating. It is, in fact, liberation. Seeing the truth is the cessation of suffering.

When the Buddha was asked how he found liberation, his answer was: discipline, concentration, and wisdom. These are called the Three Higher Trainings.

It requires wisdom to see into the very heart of reality. This kind of wisdom is far beyond the sagacity we ascribe to judges and seasoned individuals. This is the profound wisdom that sees the truth without obstruction.

Wisdom depends on a stabilized mind that is capable of focusing relentlessly on the subject. That is why the Buddha made concentration the second point. As we are now, our minds flit about like flies in a thunderstorm. Most of us lack the stability required to track the thief back to his lair. It is only by eliminating all the other possibilities of where he might be hiding that we can see once and for all that he never really existed. But we are constantly distracted in this pursuit because our minds lack the ability to maintain the intense focus required to see this search through to the end.

Our minds are swayed by inner distractions. These distractions are the result of our addiction to the delusions of anger and attachment and all their merry crew. We are constantly pulled this way and that by these negative emotions. This is why the Buddha stressed discipline. Again, this is not the ordinary discipline we might find at the hands of a school principal or a drill sergeant. The discipline here is that of the monk who stood vigilantly with his sword at the entrance to his cave. He was guarding his mind against the negative emotions. In the great scheme of liberation, this is the role of mindfulness and the purpose of this book.

Through mindfulness, we are on the trail of the thief, chasing him hard on his own horse—to free ourselves by vanquishing him once and for all by seeing the truth. The thief was never there. That is why the Buddha is smiling.

afterword
daily practice

We could benefit by a lesson from the bees. They make small but repeated efforts, day in and day out over the course of a summer. Drop by drop, they bring in the nectar of a season's worth of flowers and refine it to its essence. By working steadily, they gain a hive full of honey by the fall.

Patient, steady effort, a little each day, will lead to results. The results we are after may vary from person to person. It depends on your application and your ultimate goal. But the practice of mindfulness will reduce the power of the negative emotions. It will bring greater attention. It will bring you closer to the truth.

If you are fortunate enough to have found a path and a teacher, then you probably have some form of practice. Mindfulness is only one of the tools we use along the way. Its aim is to help us train our minds and turn them toward a positive direction.

These are some suggestions for how you can use this practice in the course of each day.

appreciation

Each day when you awake, you can appreciate the fact that you are alive, that you have one more day to work toward your benefit and that of others. You can remind yourself that this life is rare and precious and you'd like to make the best use of it while you have the opportunity.

meditation

Take a little time before you begin your day to find a quiet moment.

- *Sit quietly and steady your mind.*

- *Come back to yourself.*

- *Follow your breath.*

- *Sense yourself in your body. Feel the weight of it.*

- *Find the stillness you can return to during the day.*

Ten minutes is fine, twenty is okay. If you're fortunate to have more time and the desire to use it in this manner, wonderful.

motivation

You can begin your day as you sit by setting your motivation. How do you want to live your life? What do you wish to accomplish? These are your motivations. You may have objectives in the world, to achieve success or provide for your family. You can also have inner goals, to help yourself and others, to become more compassionate, to become more mindful.

intention

You can look ahead to the outer events of your day and set your intention for your inner work. What do you want to pay attention to? What do you wish to consider?

- *If you want to develop your attention, you can decide that you will pause each half hour to come back to your self and remember your breath or the sensation of your feet on the floor.*

- *If you are subject to anger, you can decide you want to try to see the moments when it first arises.*

- *If you are subject to pride, you might decide to catch those moments when you are advertising yourself again.*

recollection

We drift all the time, startled to find our thoughts have carried us a million miles away. As you go through the day, you can use the day's activities as a reminder to bring your attention back to the moment. Any simple act will do. Each time you sit down or stand up; each time you hear a car door slam; each time you think about your next meal. As you start out your day, you can set these "alarm clocks" in your mind to bring you back to your intention.

attention

All our activities, both negative and positive, take place in the realms of body, speech, and mind. This is where we practice mindfulness. No place else. Though we may find ourselves daydreaming about life on Mars, our work is in the here and now. Each of these realms provides opportunity for practice throughout the day. If your intention was to follow your pride, you can listen for it in the sound of your voice. You can sense it rising up in your chest. You can follow it as it turns your mind to thoughts of self-aggrandizement.

medication

In traditional teachings the Buddha is sometimes referred to as "the doctor" and the dharma or teachings as "the medicine." The illness we are trying to cure is our addiction to the negative emotions. Each of these delusions—anger, attachment, pride, jealousy, ignorance, wrong view, doubt—has an antidote. Anger is subdued by patience; attachment by understanding impermanence. Pride is countered by recognizing your limitations. Jealousy is tamed through generosity. By practicing mindfulness during the day, we can begin to recognize the symptoms and apply the antidote. Setting your intention at the beginning of the day will help you be attentive to the first sign of these symptoms.

recognition

Part of the role of mindfulness is to reduce the grasp of the ego. Through patient practice, we can begin to recognize the separation from others this grasping creates. We can use mindfulness to recognize our place in the stream of life. As human beings, we are interdependent. As you sit to eat your meal, it's a chance for you to reflect on this interconnectedness. How much effort and care were necessary for it to appear in a wholesome, nourishing form? How many people were responsible for providing your meal? Aren't they people just like you? Aren't their needs and wants the same as yours? Don't they, too, wish for happiness and freedom from suffering? What are you doing to contribute to their happiness? What are you doing that contributes to their suffering?

reflection

As your day draws to a close, take a few quiet moments to reflect on how you spent it. If you can sit still and be silent for a few minutes, all the better.

- *Review your day. Did you make good use of your precious time? Did you honor the intentions you set for yourself in the morning?*

- *Review your thoughts, your speech, and your actions during the day. Did you contribute something positive? If you did, then you can rejoice. Did you cause harm for yourself or others? If so, you can apply the four "Rs": Recognition, Regret, Resolution, and Reparation.*

- *Take stock of yourself. In Tibetan monasteries, the monks place a handful of white and black pebbles before them. They review their day's actions. For each positive act, they select a white pebble. For each negative act, they choose a black one. At the end, they take a tally. Was this day an improvement over the last?*

dedication

Before you turn in, you can dedicate your good work. You have had yet one more day of this precious life. You would like your positive efforts to be of some help and use, both for yourself and others.

checking progress

From time to time, it is both important and useful to check your progress. If you were following a path through the woods, you would look for landmarks to tell you how far you've come and whether you are still heading in the right direction. This path is no different. We need to check our progress to be sure that we are not spending our time and efforts in vain. Checking progress in this regard is quite straightforward.

- *Are your negative emotions slightly weaker than before?*

- *Are you reacting less harshly and hastily to things that used to push your buttons?*

- *Do you consider the welfare of others a little more than you used to?*

- *Do you feel more grounded within yourself, slightly less prone to having your thoughts wander here, there, and everywhere?*

- *Is it slightly easier to make time to practice?*

- *Do you find that your practice is becoming less of a burden and more of a welcome habit?*

If you find you are heading in this direction, great. If not, look into yourself to find what is getting in your way. The only thing truly standing in your way is that non-existent thief born of ignorance.

appendix
the four noble truths

Shakyamuni Buddha began his teaching with what are known as the Four Noble Truths.

The first noble truth is the truth of suffering

The Buddha taught that the nature of this life is suffering. Birth is suffering. Old age is suffering. Sickness is suffering. Death is suffering.

The second noble truth is the cause of suffering

It arises from craving. The craving is based on a profound misunderstanding of the situation. It is often called *ignorance* or not-knowing.

The third noble truth is the cessation of suffering

It is the complete cessation of that craving that binds us. It means emancipation from the bondage of suffering.

The fourth noble truth is the path that leads to freedom

It is known as the eight-fold path. It consists of eight positive activities:

- *Right view:* Seeing without delusion the truth of suffering and its cause and the cessation of suffering and its cause

- *Right aspirations:* to do good rather than evil

- *Right speech:* the avoidance of untruth, slander, harsh language, and divisive speech

- *Right action:* refraining from killing, stealing, and sexual misconduct

- *Right livelihood:* earning your living in a way that is not harmful to others

- *Right effort:* toward the good

- *Right mindfulness:* the awareness of your deeds, words and thoughts

- *Right contemplation:* the focused practice that develops a stable and concentrated mind and helps to prepare one for the ultimate attainment of wisdom and enlightenment

the buddha's last words

The Buddha had taught for forty-five years. He was now nearly eighty years old and had grown physically weaker with time. He had made his way with difficulty to Kushinagar, a place he had visited before and where many of the followers of his teachings lived. As soon as he arrived, he had his disciple Ananda prepare his bed between two sal trees. There he lay on his right side with his head to the north, facing west. He spent the first two watches of the night comforting and instructing people.

Toward the last watch, the Buddha asked his followers if they had any further questions. To Ananda's surprise, they all kept silent. Then the Buddha removed his robes and told those who remained to look upon his body. It would be the last time they would see him. Then he spoke his final words.

All component things are perishable.
Work diligently on your own salvation.